Frontispiece
Greenwich armour of Henry VIII, 1540.

MINISTRY OF PUBLIC BUILDING AND WORKS

EUROPEAN ARMOUR

IN THE TOWER OF LONDON

ARTHUR RICHARD DUFTY

Master of the Armouries

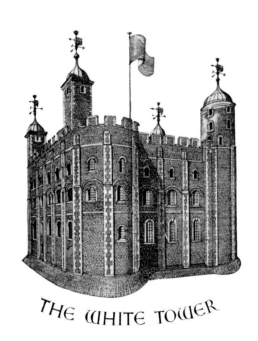

THE WHITE TOWER

LONDON: HER MAJESTY'S STATIONERY OFFICE: 1968

A

LIST OF CONTENTS

A*

In memory of
JAMES GOW MANN

PREFACE

THIS PICTURE-BOOK of European armour is the first of a series intended to illustrate selected pieces in the Armouries in Her Majesty's Tower of London. It is neither a textbook nor a catalogue, nor is it a substitute for either. The plates will be reused in a definitive catalogue of the collections which is now in preparation. A catalogue of some 2,500 pieces is necessarily expensive to produce, and this expedient will spread the cost as well as provide publications fitted to the needs of the general public and of the student.

The series will also include picture-books of European firearms and their accessories, white arms, miscellanea, and Oriental arms and armour. Publication of detailed descriptions with full references, particulars of marks and records of the provenance of the pieces must await completion of the *catalogue raisonné*.

It is fitting that this first publication of the series should be dedicated to the memory of Sir James Mann, K.C.V.O., F.B.A., F.S.A., Master of the Armouries 1939–1962, for the project was initiated by him. Unfortunately it had not progressed far at the time of his death in December, 1962. Those who knew him and shared his interest will understand the pleasure that this publication would have given him. But it is an ephemeral tribute to an eminent man. His abiding monument is the reorganisation and improvement of the Tower Armouries, by which he raised them to a high place among the armouries of the world. Their splendour and panache today is the result of his vision and love of chivalry. Without presumption Mann could well have said with Horace ' Exegi monumentum ære perennius '.

My colleagues at the Tower, Mr. A. N. Kennard, F.S.A., Mr. H. R. Robinson, F.S.A., and Mr. W. Reid, F.S.A., who have long given devoted service to the Armouries, have all helped in the preparation of this book, but particular gratitude is due to Mr. Reid who has written the Introduction. Thanks are also due to Mr. Claude Blair, F.S.A., of the Victoria & Albert Museum, for references which have been used in drafting the Introduction. Mr. Basil Marriott has been kind enough to design the vignette for the title-page.

The illustrations were prepared from photographs taken by Mr. J. H. L. Bloomfield, A.R.P.S., and Mr. F. W. Robinson of the Ministry of Public Building and Works in conditions which, initially, were never ideal and rarely better than formidable.

A. R. DUFTY
Master of the Armouries

INTRODUCTION

THE ARMOURIES in the Tower of London have the distinction of being the oldest national armoury still in the building which has always contained it. Arms and armour have been held in the Tower certainly since the close of the thirteenth century, and in all possibility since the time of William the Conqueror.

The oldest part of the fortress, the White Tower or Keep, was begun about 1078 on the north bank of the Thames, where William I immediately after his coronation had formed a stronghold, eastward of the City of London and within the angle of the old city wall first built by the Romans. It was completed in the reign of William II, presumably by 1097 and certainly by 1100, and thereafter housed the garrison that protected and controlled London, for the Tower commanded the river approach and was in daunting proximity to the City.

An enlargement of the fortress was begun late in the twelfth century, and now the White Tower is the centre of a great castle covering 18 acres. In the past the Tower of London has been a palace and a prison as well as a stronghold; it has housed the Royal Mint, the Public Records, the Royal Observatory and the Royal Menagerie. Today it houses the Crown Jewels and the Armouries.

The Armouries now comprise the residue of two great but disparate historic accumulations of the accoutrements of war and the joust, for the Tower was for centuries both the national arsenal and a repository for the equipment of our kings; in the time of Henry VIII the Tower, together with Greenwich, Westminster, Hampton Court and Windsor, housed the arms and armour belonging to the Crown, and ultimately during the Interregnum and at the Restoration in 1660 all the Royal armour from those palaces was concentrated here and at Windsor. Thus the Tower Armouries have become the nation's greatest collection of historic arms and armour. They were already a showplace long before the time of Charles II and can claim to be the oldest museum in England.

Unfortunately, the long martial history of the Tower is not matched by an equally extended series of armour and weapons representative of each epoch from the Conquest to modern times. Mediaeval armour is very much rarer than mediaeval castles and not one complete English armour survives from before the reign of Henry VIII. Mediaeval weapons are less rare and many are exhibited in the White Tower.

The present collection bears the strong impress of that most forceful and colourful of our kings, Henry VIII. In his reign the collection took shape and many of the present exhibits are due directly to his interest in arms and armour. Henry was our last mediaeval king and our first Renaissance king; his career shows that he had little interest in the Middle Ages, at the close of which he came to the throne, but he had inherited great wealth from his father, Henry VII, which he devoted to patronage on the grand scale, no doubt partly in emulation of the contemporary European sovereigns, the Emperors Maximilian I and Charles V and King Francis I.

It is perhaps not without significance that just as Maximilian, who regarded himself as the last of the knights, was deeply interested in armour and took a lead in fostering the craft by establishing new workshops, so too Henry VIII experimented with new armours and instituted royal workshops at Southwark and Greenwich. The earliest surviving products of these Tudor shops, and the earliest surviving complete armours made in England, belonged to Henry and are preserved in the Tower.

Pls. X, XII, XIV

On Henry's death in 1547 a comprehensive inventory was made that included the arms, armour, ordnance and sundry other items owned by the king and amassed in stores, forts and ships and in the palaces of England and France. The brevity of the inventory descriptions makes identification of surviving pieces now in the Tower difficult, but there can be little doubt about the *hedde pece wt a Rammes horne* and almost certainly the *Harnesse with a long bast allowr engraven and pcell guilte with Rooses and Pomegranetts* is Henry's engraved and silvered armour, which was then in the Palace of Westminster in the care of the armourer Hans Hunter, together with morions, black unpolished horse armours *as they came out of the fier*, and three hundred shields made by Hunter from old armours. The only defensive objects removed thence to the Tower from the charge of Sir Philip Hoby in Edward VI's first year were shields: eighty-four *Targetts steilde wt gonnes* and fifty-six varied targets painted with *sondry antiques*. Of these only sixteen survive at the Tower; they are of wood faced with iron with gilded or engraved decoration; those fitted with breech-loading matchlock pistols are thought to have been made about 1544–47 by Giovanbattista and his company of Ravenna, presumably for a royal bodyguard. At Greenwich were many harnesses looked after by Erasmus Kirkner, master workman at the royal workshops, and by Sir Thomas Paston; indeed, the defensive armour that occupied the gallery in the tiltyard, three *houses* and *twoo little houses* after the death of the great king must have been an imposing sight. Among the three hundred items in Kirkner's stores alone there were many armours for man and horse, of which only a fraction was destined to survive the following century. Little of it can now be identified.

Pl. LXXXII
Pls. I, XIV

Pls. CXXXVIII–CXL

The character and distribution of these stores seems to have changed little during the reigns of Edward VI and Elizabeth, allowing for the normal usage of issue and return of armour and weapons and for such conversion as that indicated by the order in 1575 to Sir George Howard, Master of the Armouries, to convert old armour into 1500 jacks (reinforced jackets) for sea service. But a major inroad into the Tower store may well have been made in 1635 when Charles I, after reserving sufficient armour for 10,000 men, ordered the rest to be sold to people in the country who had none.

By the second quarter of the seventeenth century the armourers of London appear to have made little but munition armour, and from then until the end of the Civil War no armour of distinction was brought to the Tower. But during the Interregnum, stores brought from Greenwich to London about 1644 and before 1660 included the Henry VIII armours, most of the Greenwich armours and the earlier Stuart royal armours which we see there today; these were the basis of the Armouries collection of historic as distinct from munition harnesses.

Early in Charles II's reign, no doubt as a propagandist expression of the continuity and distinction of kingship following upon the recent restoration of the monarchy, the 'Line of Kings' was set up in the Tower, which then again became a great showplace. The historical line of kings was a popular feature which, despite many glaring anachronisms, continued until well into the nineteenth century when it included at least twenty sovereigns from William the Conqueror to George II. Even allowing for Jorevin de Rocheford's hyperbole, his account of a visit to the Tower in 1672 makes impressive reading: 'The great arsenal consists of several great halls, and magazines filled with arms of all sorts, sufficient to equip an army of an hundred thousand men. Our conductor showed us a great hall, hung with casques and cuirasses for arming both infantry and cavalry; among others were some that had been worn by different kings of England in their wars; they were all gilded and engraved in the utmost perfection'. The armours seen by de Rocheford included those of Henry VIII, of courtiers of Elizabeth, of the young sons of James I and VI, and of soldiers and sailors who had fought in England's wars in Britain and overseas. Among them stood, and still stands, an unequalled collection of the works of the armourers of Greenwich.

The contents of the Tower at the time of the Restoration are known from the 1660 Inventory (Dartmouth MS in the Tower Library), and it is this Inventory which is the basis of all subsequent catalogues of the Tower Armouries. Then there were still 9,000 armours for harquebusiers, many more for cuirassiers and much of the Toiras armour. This last was brought to the Tower after the ill-fated Ile de Rhé adventure of 1627 and is first found named in the summary Inventory of 1650 (I. 56, re-acquired for the Tower, November 1963); of the thousand or so cuirasses captured, probably from the French ship *St. Esprit*, 281 breasts and backs stamped with Marshal Toiras's name are still in the Armouries and comprise the most extensive armour *Pl. CXX* trophy surviving from a seventeenth-century campaign.

For some years after 1660 armour continued to be bought for the army and received into the Tower, and a massive ledger of receipts, issues and returns exists for 1675–79. The initials of six of the armourers listed therein have been found stamped on harquebus armours; these or the initials of other unidentified craftsmen are often accompanied by the stamped hall-mark of the Armourers' Company of London, which though regularised by a Commission in 1631 was already in use certainly a generation earlier. It was a capital A surmounted by a crown or, during the late Commonwealth (1650–60), a helmet, sometimes with the shield of St. George or the crowned cypher CR or JR. Richard Hoden, one of the six armourers mentioned above, was paid £100 in 1686 for making the armour of James II, which is the latest royal harness *Pl. LXVII* now remaining in the Tower. But by the end of James II's reign the days of defensive armour were almost over. When in 1706–7 the army in Flanders required armour that would withstand a carbine shot, breasts alone were sent; these were intended to be worn in the Danish fashion, with 'cross girdle leathers'. In 1720 six dozen infantry headpieces were issued for conversion to firemen's caps, and, again, two years later 'strong' backs, breasts and pots were delivered to the furbisher in the Tower to be broken up and used in the repair of small arms.

The eighteenth century was a period of great productivity in the manufacture of firearms but was a fallow time as regards armour. Armour had gone into disuse by the beginning of the century, while scholarly study of it had still scarcely begun by the end, and even then the stimulant was the romantic association of armour rather than its interest, in an archaeological sense, its visual beauty or its functional efficacy. When Francis Grose published *A Treatise on Ancient Armour and Weapons* in 1786 he could draw for his illustrative material upon only a few British collections, apart from those at the Tower and Warwick Castle, that included some armour among the ' curiosities '. Displays of curiosities, and under this head came armour, had been mounted for a century past, and Londoners could see such collections in the ' Holophusikon ' in Leicester Square or in the ' London Museum and Pantherion ' at the Egyptian Hall. But the armour laid up in English churches, standing in ancestral homes and hanging in family armouries was still largely unrecorded: and so unfortunately it remained while revival of interest in armour and consequent increase in its value led to widespread depredations by both collectors and dealers.

With the turn of the century began a more scholarly approach to the study of arms and armour. Already by 1824 Dr. Samuel Rush Meyrick, one of the earliest and greatest *amateurs d'armes*, had offered advice to the Duke of Wellington upon improvements in the display of the armour in the Tower, and thereafter the Principal Storekeeper consulted him regarding the purchase of armour. In 1826 he was invited to supervise the arrangement in the New Horse Armoury just then completed. He reorganised the ' Line of Kings ', changing such solecisms as William the Conqueror in a Greenwich armour of about 1585 for something of his own creation, more accurate than the Restoration group though still fanciful. For his work at the Tower and at Windsor he received the Guelphic Order of Knighthood from George IV.

Pl. XLVI

The publication of Meyrick's classic *A Critical Inquiry into Antient Armour* in 1824 (2nd edn. 1842) and the creation of his own large private collection at Goodrich Court in Herefordshire encouraged intelligent interest in the subject; antiquarian societies began to regard armour as a reputable object of study, and the Tower subsequently acquired a number of pieces which had been exhibited before the Society of Antiquaries.

One of the unsung heroes of the Armouries was Robert Porrett, F.R.S., F.S.A., Chief Clerk under the Principal Storekeeper to the Board of Ordnance, son of Robert Porrett, an Ordnance Storekeeper. The Board were the governing authority in the Tower and about 1825 Porrett persuaded them to buy for the national collection. This was highly commendable, and important pieces were bought. It was only unfortunate that Samuel Luke Pratt of Bond Street and Lower Grosvenor Street, the most important dealer of his day, and the supplier of the armour for the rain-sodden Eglinton Tournamest of 1839, was at the time passing much fake armour through the auction rooms, where, at Christie's, Deacon's and Oxenham's, the picturesque if totally dishonest genealogies attached thereto satisfied the romantic tastes of the buyers. But if fakes thus came to the Tower they were more than compensated for by such acquisitions, in which Porrett had a hand, as the Stowe helm from a British source and, in 1826 and again possibly in 1846, quantities of Italian munition armour of the late sixteenth and early seventeenth centuries brought from Malta which have made the Armouries an important centre for the study of this material.

Pl. LXXXIII

In a Christie's sale of 1839 the Tower bought a number of pieces stolen from the Real Armeria in Madrid, which have subsequently been identified from the *Inventario Iluminado* as having come from the great armoury of the Emperor Charles V; in 1840 the Oddi armour now at Windsor and the Tower 'Pisan' horse armour were bought from Pratt, and a year later were acquired parts of an early sixteenth-century parade armour simulating the puffed and slashed civilian costume then in fashion. This was the year, 1841, when the Grand Storehouse in the Tower was burned down.

Pls. CXXVIII, CXXIX

Many purchases were made in the following decade at the instigation of Porrett, and they were paid for out of the visitors' entrance fees. It seems that from about 1840 to 1851 the entire proceeds were devoted to the wages of the attendants, some £800 annually, and to purchases: a happy state of affairs which has never recurred.

Porrett retired in 1850; nonetheless purchases were made each year from 1851 to 1855. In the latter year many pieces were bought at the Bernal sale, including the helmet of Sir Henry Lee, Master of the Armouries 1578–1610, and a fine fifteenth-century shield from Zwickau in Bohemia. Though little money seems to have been allocated for purchases during the rest of the century, the precedent set by Porrett, with his fortunate love of antiquity combined with power of persuasion over the establishment, ensured a policy of adding fine pieces to the collection in the Armouries by purchase or by gift, whether or not they had any historical or traditional connection with the Tower of London. Unfortunately, the records for the period are incomplete, and it is not always possible to distinguish between old Tower stores and nineteenth-century accessions.

Pl. XCV
Pl. CXXXVIa

With the improvement in the Armouries, which was itself the expression of a more enlightened attitude to the collection, there came an equally logical improvement in the catalogues and guides to the Tower and its contents. J. R. Planché and J. Hewitt each contributed to the accuracy and authority of the series which appeared before the appointment in 1892 of the Hon. Harold Dillon, later Viscount Dillon, as the first Curator of the Armouries. He was one of the leading armour scholars of his day and his catalogue, published in 1910, shows a further marked advance in scholarship largely as a result of his own original researches. It is historically fitting that Dillon should have been a direct descendant of Sir Henry Lee, who was Master of the Armouries in the reign of Elizabeth I.

In 1913 Lord Dillon was succeeded as Curator by Charles ffoulkes. With the duties, ffoulkes inherited a chronic lack of funds for making purchases, a state of affairs which lasted for a quarter of a century, and an official attitude towards the payment of the staff that had been conditioned by Dillon's altruistic retention of amateur status: he had accepted no fee for his services as Curator. Nevertheless in 1916 ffoulkes published through the Stationery Office his two-volume *Inventory and Survey of the Armouries of the Tower of London*, which remains the fullest published catalogue of the collection; in its compilation he had the assistance of his predecessor's vast assembly of notes.

Pl. XVII

During ffoulkes' tenure no major additions to the collection were made between the end of the War and 1927, but in the latter year some very fine pieces came to the Tower on transfer from the Rotunda at Woolwich, then under the care of the Royal Artillery Institution. The so-called 'Bayard' armour, a part of the considerable quantity of arms and armour that had been removed from Paris in 1815, was the only complete harness, but among the headpieces were two of outstanding quality and importance: the *Pl. LXXXVI* Brocas helm and the close helmet now numbered IV. 412. The Brocas helm, an English jousting helm, named after an erstwhile owner, helped to fill a serious gap in the collection; to this day it and the Stowe helm are the only defences of their kind in the Armouries, other than the grotesque forgeries bought in the middle of the last century. *Pl. XCa* The splendid engraved, etched and gilded close helmet with fluted skull and boldly roped comb is perhaps the most pleasing object transferred and is fit to stand with any other of its style and date in existence. Also of the finest craftsmanship are the tail-piece *Pl. CLVI* from a horse-armour by the Nuremberg master Kunz Lochner and a shoulder shield *Pl. CXXXIII* from the armour garniture now in Vienna made for the Emperor Maximilian II (1527–76) by Franz Grosschedel of Landshut in 1571. But students of Italian armour may consider that the outstanding part of the transfer is the collection of early material brought from the Castle of Rhodes; this the Turks had presumably captured from the Christian garrison with the island in 1523. The hoard comprises breast and backplates, *Pls. VI, LXXVII, LXXIX, LXXX, CX–CXIII* leg harness, pauldrons, visors, a fine chanfron and important helmets; these last include an armet and a group of sallets.

In May 1935 the ancient title of *Master of the Armouries* was revived after being in abeyance since 1668. Charles ffoulkes, previously Curator, became the first of the new Masters. In 1939 he was succeeded by James Gow Mann. Mann's first acquisition was *Pl. XXXVIII* bought in May 1939; this, a fine three-quarter armour, was the most notable harness that came to the Armouries between the Wars. It was made in the royal workshops at Greenwich probably for William Herbert, 1st Earl of Pembroke (1501?–1570), and was preserved at Wilton, the seat of the Earls of Pembroke, as part of the only private armoury of a great British noble family surviving to modern times. This armoury, of the highest historical and archaeological interest, was dispersed more or less unrecorded in three sales held in 1921, 1922 and 1923. The Tower harness then passed into the collection of William Randolph Hearst, the American newspaper magnate, from whom it was bought for the Armouries through the generosity of the National Art-Collections Fund. A number of pieces given in 1942 by Mr. F. H. Cripps-Day also *Pls. LXII, LXV, CVI* came from Wilton, and so did Pembroke retainers' armour and miscellanea obtained from Major H. D. Barnes by gift and purchase.

Cripps-Day's gift, one of several he made, also included a small collection of spurs, to which have since been added important examples from the Francis Mallet (1947),

W. R. Hearst (1952) and C. R. Beard (1958) collections. These extend the series of spurs, almost all of unknown provenance, which was in the Armouries at the time of publication of the 1915 *Inventory and Survey*. The assemblage, though still modest, includes the earliest relics in the Armouries, some antedating the White Tower itself; among them, the eleventh-century Chardstock spurs are possibly the finest surviving examples of the kind. Though scarcely to be classified as armour, spurs are so symbolic of the armed panoply of chivalry that the opportunity has been taken to illustrate a number of them in this picture book.

Pls. CLX–CLXIV

Pl. CLX

In December 1942 came the receipt by the Armouries of the most important single accession since the seventeenth century: the Norton Hall Collection. Through the National Art-Collections Fund, the nation acquired *en bloc* the arms and armour brought together in the middle of the nineteenth century by Beriah Botfield, the younger, and kept at Norton Hall near Daventry. Much of the armour was collected in the early 1840s, as several items can be identified in the catalogues of the sales held then at Deacon's and Oxenham's rooms. Though defensive armour does not form the finest part of the collection, it includes a number of interesting suits, one said to be from the ducal armoury at Lucca. A pastiche of a fifteenth-century armour, almost certainly assembled by Samuel Pratt, included a good Italian sallet and a breastplate decorated with a unicorn among clouds; these are now exhibited separately. An etched and gilt plackart with the firesteels of the Order of the Golden Fleece is probably the one recorded in the *Inventario Iluminado*. Botfield's collection was one of a number of contemporary collections formed in the afterglow of Walter Scott's Romanticism, many of which, including those of Lord Zouche at Parham, Lord Brougham and Vaux at Brougham, Sir Archibald Lamb at Battle and John Beardmore at Uplands, were dispersed in a series of sales that followed the first World War. Fortunately, at this period when absence of funds left the Armouries powerless to compete against rich and active foreign buyers, the Botfield collection remained at Norton Hall. Circumstances were more propitious for the Tower when it came on the market in the year 1942.

Pl. LXI
Pl. CVIII

Pl. CXXXII

Against such a gain must be set the two tragic losses to the Tower Armouries at the time of the nadir in its resources in the 1920s, and when still no check had been set by the State upon the export of works of art of national importance. The Pembroke and Cumberland armours, two of the finest examples of the work of the royal armourers at Greenwich, the first made for Henry Herbert, 2nd Earl of Pembroke, K.G. (1534–1601), the second for George Clifford, Earl of Cumberland, K.G. (1558–1605), were sold and went abroad: today, licences for their export would be refused and grants be sought for their purchase for the Tower. But not all the fine armour that went abroad between the two Wars has remained there. Part of the Clarence Mackay collection was sent from America to be sold a few weeks before the outbreak of the 1939–45 War at Christie's, where Sir Archibald Lyle bought the superlative fourteenth-century bascinet from Schloss Churburg in the Tirol. In 1946 Sir Archibald bequeathed it to the Armouries in memory of his sons, Captain I. A. de H. Lyle,

Pl. LXXII

Black Watch, killed at El Alamein in 1942 and Major R. A. Lyle, Scottish Horse, killed in Normandy in June, 1944.

Pls. XXVI, XXVII, LIII
Pl. LXIX

Apart from the little Stuart armours which have been Tower exhibits since the seventeenth century, there were no armours for children in the collection until 1948 when two, for boys of about eight and ten years respectively, were bequeathed to the nation by Sir Bernard Eckstein. These two harnesses, apparently made by the same Augsburg maker about 1610, were meant for wearing when practising a form of foot combat with sword or pike over a low barrier separating the contestants. Both came

Pl. LXVIII

from the armoury of the Duke of Saxe-Altenburg at Altenburg. A third harness, made for a child of about eight years, was bought in 1950; it has blued surfaces with gilt bands and borders and was formerly in the Earl of Londesborough and E. J. Brett collections. But the most notable boy's armour to be acquired in modern times is the

Pls. XXXVI, XXXVII

Greenwich three-quarter armour which was the property of Lord Mount Edgecumbe until its purchase from Cotehele in 1957. When it was first brought to the Armouries a thick coating of black paint and the rigid effect of the wooden figure to which it was nailed combined to give the impression that it was no more than a coarse wooden statuette. Cleaning revealed a delightfully proportioned and technically excellent armour with a laminated cuirass of *anime* type and gilt borders. This is the third *anime* only to be identified as of Greenwich make. Unfortunately it lacks helmet and gauntlets.

Pl. CXXXV

In 1949 a finely modelled, embossed buffe signed by the brothers Filippo and Francesco Negroli and dated 1538 was added to the Italian pieces in the collection. This was about the time that the decision was made to acquire for the Tower painted portraits that would show how armour was worn. The first such acquisition under

Pl. XLVII

this plan was the portrait of Robert Radcliffe, 5th Earl of Sussex (1569?–1629), in a Greenwich armour, bought in 1950. Among those since obtained are the very fine

Pl. CXXIV
Pl. LXXI

portrait of Sir John Robinson in buff coat and cuirass by John Michael Wright and one of a series painted in Rubens's studio for the Palais de Luxembourg.

In 1952 came the most important acquisition made by the Armouries since the Restoration and one unlikely to be equalled. This was the purchase, with help from the Pilgrim Trust, the National Art-Collections Fund and a Special Exchequer Grant, of much of the armour and weapons from that part of the William Randolph Hearst collection which was housed in St. Donat's Castle, Glamorganshire. Not only are the pieces of the finest quality in themselves, but, fortunately, they fill several serious

Pls. VIII, IX

gaps in the national collections. The most impressive single armour is that made for the court of the Emperor Maximilian I, for use in the joust known as the *Scharfrennen*, in which the contestants aimed to unhorse each other but where points were also gained for lances broken. This fine example from the Imperial Armoury, Vienna, shows all

Pl. VII

that was best in the Innsbruck armourers' craft. A composite Gothic armour comes from Churburg, and other harnesses and helmets are from dynastic collections including those of the kings of Saxony, Count Erbach and the Duke of Ratibor.

Pl. CXXVI

The earliest Hearst pieces are a bascinet skull and a mail shirt, both of the fourteenth century. According to tradition, the shirt belonged to Rudolf IV, Duke of Austria and Styria (1339–65). It is an excellent example of mail-maker's technique, using alternate rows of welded and riveted rings. A German cuirass etched with a Crucifix and a kneeling knight still retains its original lining of fine chamois leather. This last and another original lining in a Dresden tilt armour bear their owners' names inscribed in black ink. Among the four chanfrons, one enriched with an etched design in the so-called *fico* style belongs to the armour No. 20 in the Kretzschmar von Kienbusch collection in New York; another, from Churburg, still has its fifteenth-century linen lining.

Pl. XXVIII

Pl. LVII
Pl. CXLV

Pl. CXLIV

Very generously in 1953 the Hearst Corporation presented from the same collection the defensive coat of thick buff leather once owned by Colonel Francis Hacker, who was on the scaffold to supervise the execution of Charles I. His defence for the part he took in the king's death, ' I was a soldier, and under command ', has been echoed countless times since his trial on 15th October, 1660.

Pl. CXXV

The ranks of armours in the White Tower were also supplemented in 1953 by six harnesses lent by the 2nd Duke of Westminster from his small collection at Eaton Hall in Cheshire, where it had been since the last century. These include two good Augsburg tilting armours, a fine cuirass and tassets from an etched and gilt Nuremberg field armour of about 1550, and a composite but interesting fluted armour. The six became part of the permanent collection in the Armouries when acquired from the Westminster estate in 1959.

Pl. LVI
Pl. XXXIII
Pl. XVI

Not all important acquisitions have come from famous collections however. A mail shirt, previously unknown and unrecorded, was sent to the Armouries for examination in 1957 and found to have lettered brass rings incorporated into the fabric of the mail which identified it as the product of an Iserlohn mail-maker who was active about 1400. It was bought for the Tower, any armour of that early date of which the maker has been recognised being significant. Important pieces have thus emerged from obscurity and been acquired; others, bought or received as gifts from generous private donors since 1939, were previously known only from sale catalogues and books published since the first edition of Grose's *Treatise*.

Pl. CXXVI

Few sights are more evocative of valour, chivalry and dignity than that of an armed man on an armed horse; this association stems from inherited Romanticism, and surely too from the impression of bravery personified conveyed by representations of St. George mounted and armed *cap-à-pied* spearing the dragon. But genuine early horse armour is of the greatest rarity. Of the six such armours known to survive from the fifteenth century in any degree of completeness only one, that possibly made for the Duke Waldemar VI of Anhalt-Zerbst, was still in private possession in 1958. In that year it was acquired for the Armouries through the generosity of the National Art-Collections Fund. Thus once again the Fund obtained a major work of craftsmanship of the utmost rarity for the nation. In the *ensemble* now exhibited the armour for the man and the saddle do not belong to the Waldemar horse armour, but they are contemporary with it.

Pls. II, III

The foregoing brings the story of major acquisitions to very recent years, but two notable accessions which deserve special mention have since come to the Tower. The Electress Sophia, wife of the Elector Christian I of Saxony, intending to present her husband with a sumptuous Christmas gift, placed an order with Anton Peffenhauser for twelve identical armours richly blued, etched and gilt for the combat on foot over the barrier. But the Elector's death in September 1591 preceded the gift, and the armours were delivered to his widow at Dresden; and there six remain. Of the other six, one

Pls. LIV, LV

which had been in the Clarence Mackay collection was bought for the Armouries in June 1959. It is an outstanding example of the later work of the master, Peffenhauser, who dominated the Augsburg armourers for forty years. The second more recent

Pl. XXXI

acquisition, from the collection of the 10th Duke of Northumberland, is an armour which was made in one of the South German workshops for a member of the Hirnheim family of Swabia; this identification is proved by the heraldic escutcheons on the two chanfrons from the same garniture which are in the Wallace Collection and the Musée de Cluny. It is illustrated here as it was brought from Alnwick Castle in 1960 and as reunited with its extra pieces now in the Wallace Collection (A.43).

However, this story is not one of consistent growth and improvement. Some of the vicissitudes of the Armouries have been described; further, from time to time the stores of arms and armour held in the Tower were depleted by sales, such as those held in 1687, 1717 and 1924, and by transfers for the decoration of public buildings and royal residences, the Banqueting House in Whitehall, Hampton Court Palace, Windsor Castle and the Prince Regent's home in Carlton House. Not all of these issues were returned and occasionally they resulted in the pieces of an armour being separated, to be brought together again only by a combination of good fortune and professional knowledge. Over a period of three years the staff of the Armouries reunited the tilt armour

Pl. XXXIV

II. 188, pieces being found in Windsor Castle, Dover Castle and the Tower. Further causes of loss and damage arose from the practice of lending armour to artists as studio props and to producers for stage plays. Was it more than chance, for example, that the armour lent to B. R. Haydon, the historical painter, for a picture he was painting for Lord Mulgrave in 1808 ever returned to the Tower? Worse still were the loans to the men who trailed their pikes through a November London in the Lord Mayor's Show. These were discouraged after 1877 when the City Remembrancer was recommended to obtain reproduction armours instead of those previously borrowed from the Tower.

Pl. XXIV

Had this recommendation been made earlier, the colossal harness in the Armouries once erroneously known as that of 'John of Gaunt' might now be in a better state of preservation.

On one occasion at least, parts of a unique royal armour were issued to be worn by the King's Champion at a Coronation. The office of Champion has been hereditary in the Dymoke family since 1377; the family seat is at Scrivelsby in Lincolnshire, and there in 1947 were identified the leg defences engraved with the Garter from the Tower

Pls. X, XI

tonlet armour of Henry VIII. They have now been returned to complete the harness.

Thus the chronicle of the Armouries comes back full cycle to Henry VIII. This is not fortuitous. Henry loved fine armour. He did not collect, as we understand the expression, and as Ferdinand of the Tyrol collected in the next generation, but long after his death the Armouries developed into an historic collection when the Tower became the repository of the armours which had been made to his order, or presented to him, and of the armours made in the Greenwich workshops which he began. He is therefore the presiding genius, and his own four armours still standing in the White Tower even suggest his presence! The power and truculency of the man we know from history are there, rounded out, in the ' big ' armour of 1540.

Frontispiece

Essentially, however, the Tower is an arsenal; such it was at the Restoration when armour had become obsolete; so it still was in the first quarter of the nineteenth century when the Board of Ordnance reduced the quantity of armour in store by reissuing old cuirasses to certain cavalry regiments, or in 1821 when the Royal Horse Guards received an issue of seventeenth-century troopers' cuirasses then recently faced with sheet brass. *Pl. CXXI* The best surviving example of such ancient function is at Graz, where the arsenal remains a vast mobilisation store, unaltered and almost undepleted, as it was in the seventeenth century. At Berne too the old arsenal was the nucleus of the present eclectic collection.

Thus the Tower Armouries, so typical of our national continuity and empiricism, combine both arsenal and historic collection. Accessions of choice and rare armour and weapons over the last century have accentuated the latter aspect, an aspect which must too predominate in this picture book; but still in 1925 that distinguished scholar, F. H. Cripps-Day, was quite truthfully able to write ' The Tower of London still retains much of its character as an arsenal, and we are glad that this is so '. By future rearrangement it is hoped to convey more clearly this ancient characteristic of the Tower.

WILLIAM REID

a

b

Henry VIII's engraved and silvered armour (II. 5) of *c.* 1514, probably made by Italian craftsmen working in England (*see also* Plates XIV, XV, LXXXI, CXLI). Matching bard (VI. 1–5); Flemish *c.* 1514–*c.* 1519. Mark (*a*) stamped on helmet bowl, (*b*) on peytral.

PLATE I

B*

a
b
c

Horse armour (VI. 379) probably made for Waldemar VI of Anhalt–Zerbst (1450–1508); German, late 15th century. Composite armour for man (II. 3), with mark (*a*) of Jörg Treytz of Innsbruck stamped on sallet (Plate LXXIX), (*b*) on breast, (*c*) on each greave, both unidentified; late 15th century.

PLATE II

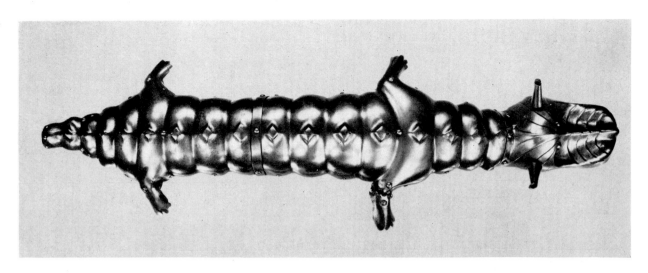

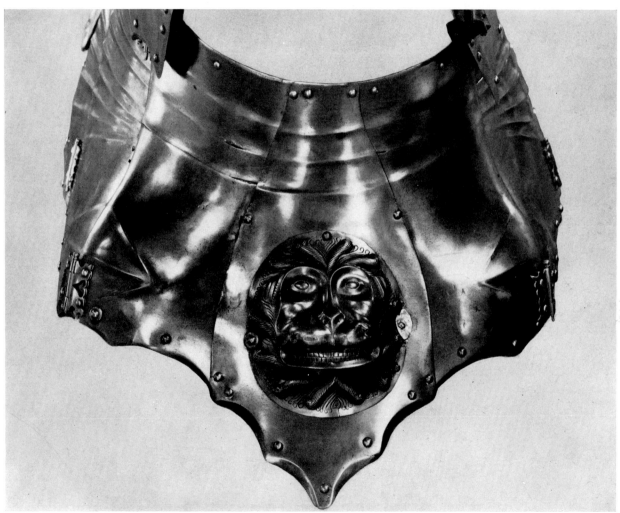

Details of horse armour opposite; tail piece (*above*) in form of monster;
peytral (*below*).

PLATE III

Greenwich armour (11.8) of Henry VIII, dated 1540, Greenwich saddle-steels (VI. 96-7), *c.* 1540, and European horse-armour (VI. 13-16), early 16th century, shown prior to dismounting in 1963. (*See* Plate XVIII.)

PLATE IV

Horse armour (VI 34, 65, 77, 84) and composite armour for man (II. 2),
with Nuremberg marks stamped on both helmet (Plate XCI) and gorget;
German (Nuremberg), c. 1510–20.

PLATE V

Left: Armour composed largely of pieces from Rhodes (III. 1011–2, 1083, 1122–3, etc.), with some restoration; Italian armourers' marks (*a, b, c*) on pauldrons, (*d*) on right couter; mid and late 15th century.

Right: Composite field armour (II. 1), with maker's mark (*a*) on breast and (*b*) of Klaus Wagner of Innsbruck on cuisses; German, late 15th century.

PLATE VI

Field armour (II. 168) composed largely of pieces from the Armoury at Churburg; unidentified marks (*a*) on sallet (Plate LXXVI), (*c*) on breast, (*d*) on pauldrons, (*e*) on cuisses; mark (*b*) of Giovanni dei Barini of Milan on bevor; Italian, Milanese, *c.* 1480; leg harness mid 15th century; right gauntlet modern.

PLATE VII

Tilt armour (*Rennzeug*) (II. 167) for form of joust with sharp
lances, known as *Rennen*; Innsbruck (?), *c.* 1490, made for
Court of Emperor Maximilian I (1459–1519).   From the
Imperial Armoury, Vienna.   (*See opposite.*)

PLATE VIII

Front, with targe and vamplate removed.

Left side (with modern lance truncated for display).

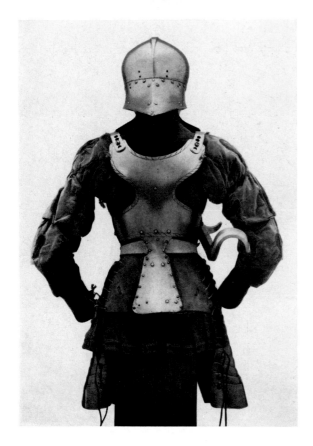

Details of *Rennzeug* opposite (*see also* Plates CXXXIII, CXLV).

Back, with targe and vamplate removed.

PLATE IX

Henry VIII's armour (II. 7) for fighting on foot; marks of Milanese Missaglia armourers stamped on helmet; the rest perhaps made by Italian craftsmen working in England, c. 1512. Gauntlets associated.

PLATE X

Details of engraved decoration on Henry VIII's armour (*opposite*): medallion of Virgin and Child on helmet-skull; Collar of the Order of the Garter; Tudor roses and foliage on tonlet. Engraver's fleur-de-lys mark.

PLATE XI

PLATE XII

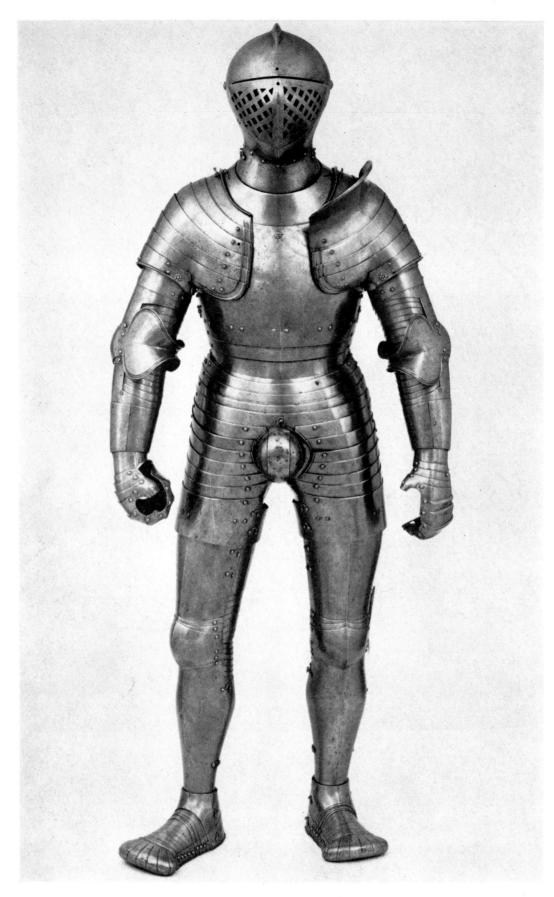

Henry VIII's armour for foot combat (II. 6); English, made
c. 1515–20 in the Royal Workshops at Greenwich; front view.

Henry VIII's foot-combat armour (*opposite*); back view.
(*See also* Plate LXXXVII.)

PLATE XIII

Armour (II. 5) of King Henry VIII probably made by Filippo de Grampis and
Giovanni Angelo de Littis, Italian armourers working in England, *c.* 1514.
Engraving, silvering and gilding of entire surfaces by Paul van Vrelant, a
Flemish artist employed as king's 'Harness gilder'.
(*See also* Plates I, XV, LXXXI, CXLI.)

PLATE XIV

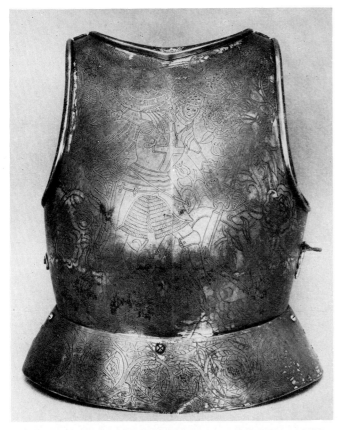

Details of Henry VIII's engraved, silvered and gilded armour (*opposite*). Breast-plate engraved with figure of St. George. Unidentified maker's mark stamped on helmet skull. Royal initials H (for Henry) and K (for Katherine) in brass on border of base. Left leg harness engraved with badges of King Henry VIII (roses) and Queen Katherine (pomegranates).

PLATE XV

C

a

b

Half armour (II. 171), painted black with red cross on breast; stamped with Nuremberg marks, (*a*) outside, (*b*) inside; German, Nuremberg, *c.* 1510.

Fluted armour (II. 179), stamped with Nuremberg mark; German, Nuremberg, *c.* 1520.

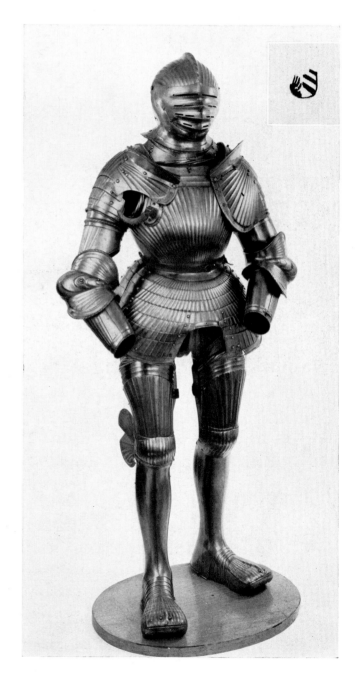

PLATE XVI

Armour (II. 135), made up of pieces from two armours; by tradition that of Chevalier Bayard (1473?–1524), but the evidence is lacking; French or Italian, c. 1520.

a

b

Armour (II. 4) with Nuremberg marks, (*a*) outside, (*b*) inside; with associated helmet; German, Nuremberg, c. 1530.

Plate XVII

c*

Part of Henry VIII's armour garniture (II. 8), with recessed, etched and gilt borders, shown here assembled for use in the foot combat; English, made in Royal Workshops at Greenwich, dated 1540; front view. (*Ref.* Frontispiece, Plates IV, XVIII–XXIII.)

PLATE XVIII

Part of Henry VIII's armour garniture (*see opposite*); back view.

PLATE XIX

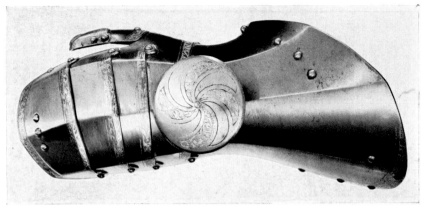

Bridle gauntlet.

Corset frontal plate,
strapped tight to chest
and midriff to provide
close-fitting support for
cuirass bolted to it.

Detail of helmet and
grandguard.

Locking gauntlet.

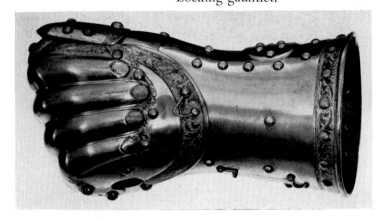

Parts of Henry VIII's Greenwich armour
garniture (II. 8), dated 1540.
(*Ref.* Frontispiece, Plates XVIII–XXIII.)

PLATE XX

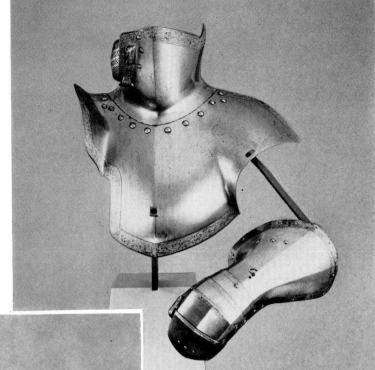

Henry VIII's 1540 Greenwich garniture (*see opposite*): extra pieces for tilt.

Grandguard and bridle gauntlet.

Second grandguard, pasguard, vambrace, bridle gauntlet, tassets, etc.

PLATE XXI

Helmet, 1540; shown here with tilt visor and with associated gorget plates.

Helmet, 1540; shown here with foot combat visor and without associated gorget plates removed 1964.

Falling buffe from field helmet, second quarter 16th century.

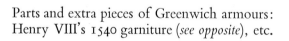
Parts and extra pieces of Greenwich armours: Henry VIII's 1540 garniture (*see opposite*), etc.

PLATE XXII

Arm defences.

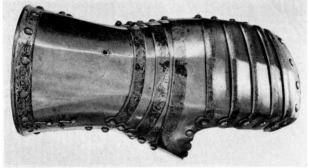

Mitten gauntlet, one of pair.

Locking gauntlet.

Henry VIII's Greenwich garniture (II. 8) of 1540 (*ref.* Frontispiece, Plates XVIII–XXIII).

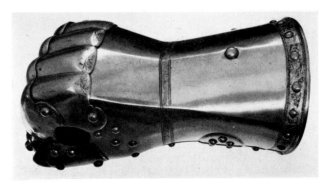

PLATE XXIII

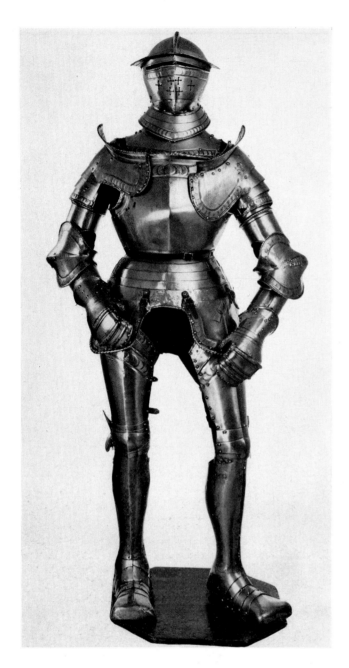

Armour (II. 22), with borders of embossed and etched scales including etcher's initials AB; for a man about 6 ft. 9 ins. tall; North German (Brunswick ?), c. 1540.

Field armour (II. 29), with etching in typical style associated with the Court of the Dukes of Brunswick; German, c. 1540; (above) detail of frieze on breast.

PLATE XXIV

Light horseman's armour (II. 31), with embossed borders; North German, mid 16th century.

Below: Light cavalry armour (II. 23), with the mark of Michel Witz the younger; Innsbruck, *c.* 1540.

Below: Armour (II. 33), with Nuremberg marks and a maker's mark incorporating the initials HM, *c.* 1540.

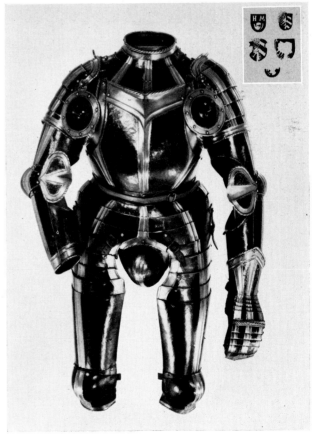

PLATE **XXV**

Armour (II. 88), traditionally but wrongly known as that of Prince Henry, son of James I, 1594–1612, decorated with blued and gilt bands; French or Italian, early 17th century. (*See also* Plate XXVII.)

Parade armour (II. 89), embossed with lions' masks and damascened with foliate patterns in gold (*see also* Plates XXVII, XCVI); French or Italian, *c.* 1540–50.

PLATE XXVI

Gorget, *c.* 1610, associated with armour (II. 89) *opposite*.

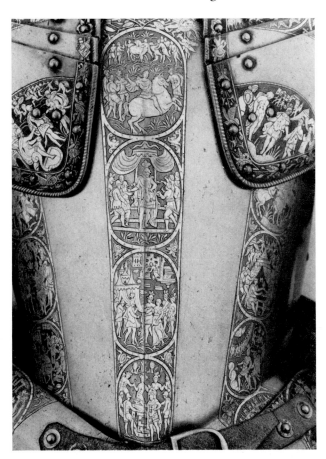

Details of enrichment of breasts of armours (II. 88, 89) *opposite*.

PLATE XXVII

Close helmet, gorget and cuirass (II. 173), with etched decoration; probably
Innsbruck, *c.* 1560.

Plate XXVIII

Close helmet, cuirass and arm defences (II. 172), decorated with etched and gilt borders (*see also* Plate CXXXII); perhaps Augsburg, *c.* 1560. From the Imperial Armoury, Vienna.

PLATE XXIX

Portrait (I. 54) of Fernando Alvarez, Duke of Alba, wearing armour of
c. 1560 and Collar of the Order of the Golden Fleece; artist unknown.

PLATE XXX

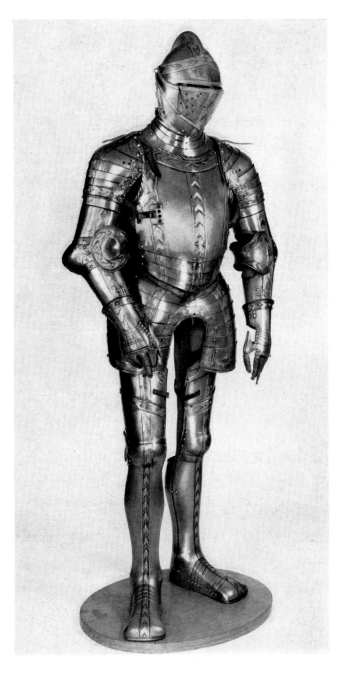

The same armour (II. 187) shown fitted with extra pieces now in the Wallace Collection (A. 43).

Armour (II. 187), with etched and gilt bands embossed with chevrons; South German, *c.* 1550 (with some modern restoration). Made for a member of the Hirnheim family of Swabia.

PLATE XXXI

D

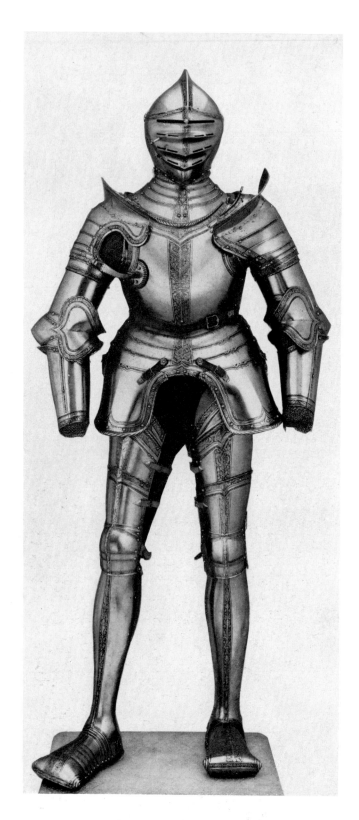

Field armour (II. 169); with detail of etched decoration on breast; Innsbruck, dated 1549.

PLATE XXXII

Parts of field armour (II. 183); with detail of etched and gilt decoration on breast; German, probably Nuremberg, c. 1550.

PLATE XXXIII

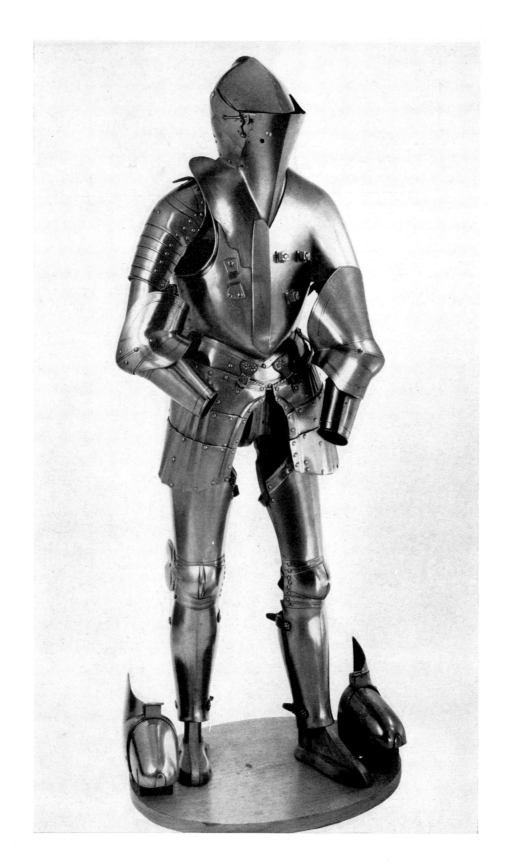

Tilt armour (II. 188); North Italian, *c.* 1560.

PLATE XXXIV

Tilt pieces of etched and gilt armour (II. 145); German, probably Augsburg, *c.* 1570–80.

PLATE **XXXV**

Three-quarter armour (II. 178) with *anime* (*i.e.* laminated) cuirass and gilt borders, for boy about twelve years of age; made in Royal Workshops at Greenwich, *c.* 1550.

PLATE XXXVI

Inside of back, showing straps, sliding rivets and attached rear plates of gorget.

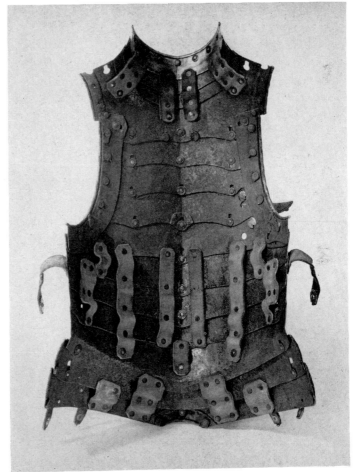

Inside of breast, showing straps and sliding rivets, gussets and attached front plates of gorget.

Boy's three-quarter armour (*see opposite*): construction of *anime* cuirass.

PLATE XXXVII

Three-quarter armour (II. 137), made, perhaps for William Herbert, 1st Earl of Pembroke (1501?–70), in Royal Workshops at Greenwich, c. 1550, right gauntlet modern.   From Armoury of Earls of Pembroke at Wilton House.

PLATE XXXVIII

Portrait (I. 46) of Henry Hastings, 3rd Earl of Huntingdon, wearing armour possibly made *c.* 1560 in Royal Workshops at Greenwich for his brother-in-law, Robert Dudley, Earl of Leicester. Dated 1588.

PLATE XXXIX

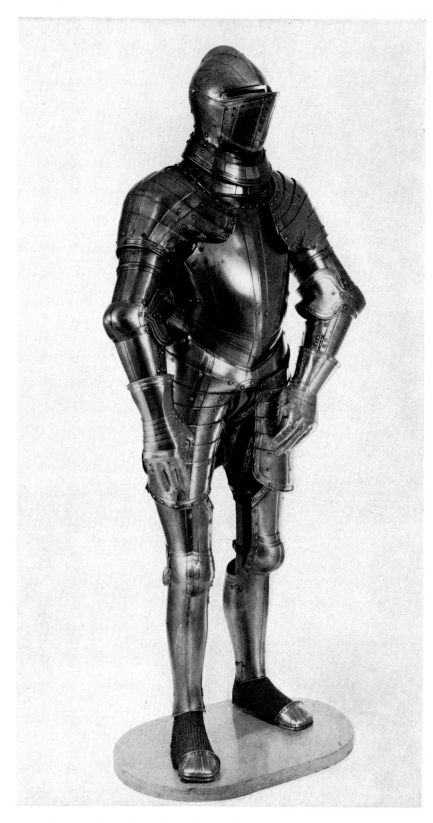

Armour (II. 82), with sunk and gilded bands; made in Royal
Workshops at Greenwich, *c.* 1550, gauntlets modern.

PLATE XL

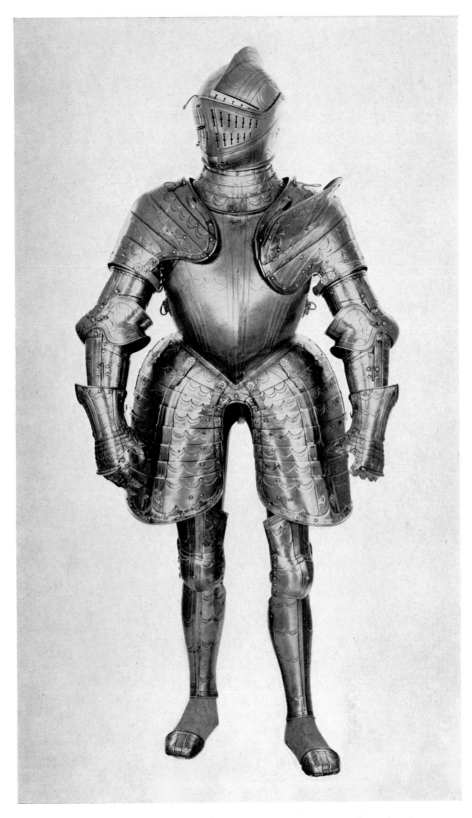

Armour (II. 83) of William Somerset, K.G., 3rd Earl of
Worcester (1526–89), originally blued with gilt scallops;
made in Royal Workshops at Greenwich, *c.* 1570–80. (*See
also* Plates XLII, XLIII.)

PLATE XLI

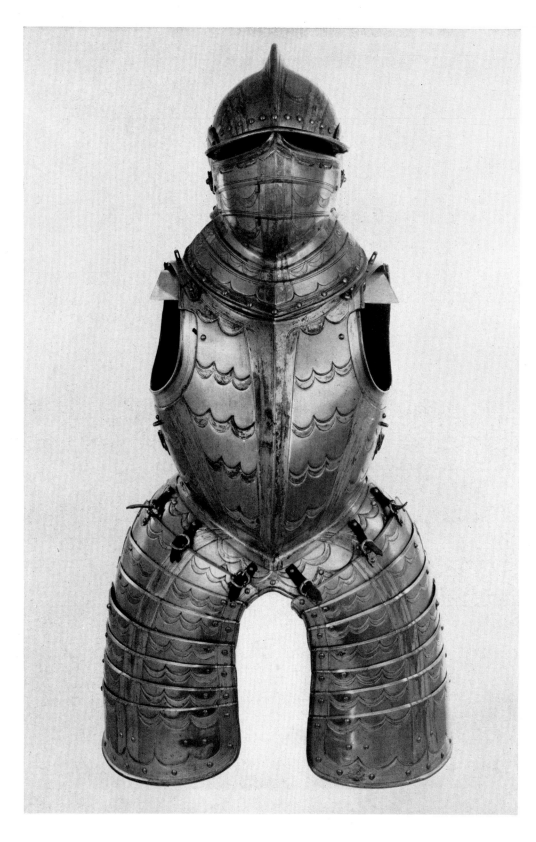

Greenwich armour (II. 83) of William Somerset, K.G., 3rd Earl of Worcester:
extra burgonet and cuirass, etc.; *c.* 1570–80 (*see also* Plates XLI, XLIII).

PLATE XLII

Burgonet with falling buffe.

Reinforcing breast with lance-rest.

Half chanfron (VI. 50).

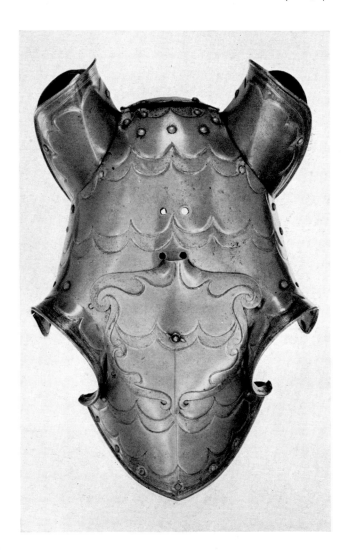

Extra pieces of Worcester's armour (*see opposite*).

PLATE XLIII

Armour (II. 81) of Robert Dudley, K.G., Earl of Leicester (1532?–88), embossed, etched and gilt; decoration including bears and ragged staves, for Warwick, and Dudley's initials RD; etched on breast, lesser George and French Order of *Saint Michel;* made in Royal Workshops at Greenwich, *c.* 1575. (*See also* Plates XLV, XCIV.)

PLATE XLIV

Grandguard.

Chanfron (VI. 49).

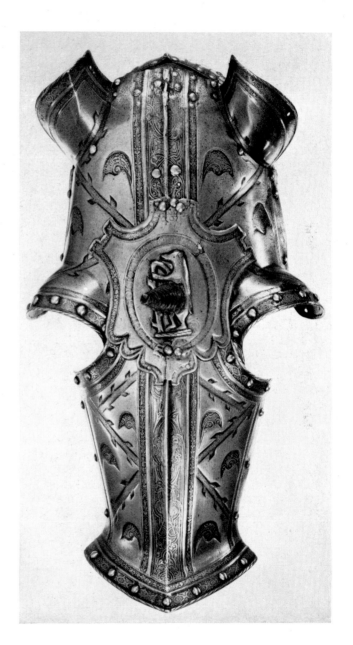

Pasguard.

Leicester's armour (*see opposite and* Plate XCIV): extra pieces etc.

PLATE XLV

Field and tilt armour (II. 40); made in Royal Workshops at Greenwich, c. 1585. Long popularly known as the armour of William the Conqueror!

PLATE XLVI

Portrait (I. 36) of Robert Radcliffe, 5th Earl of Sussex (1569?–1629), in Greenwich armour for foot combat over a barrier; painted in 1593.

PLATE XLVII

E

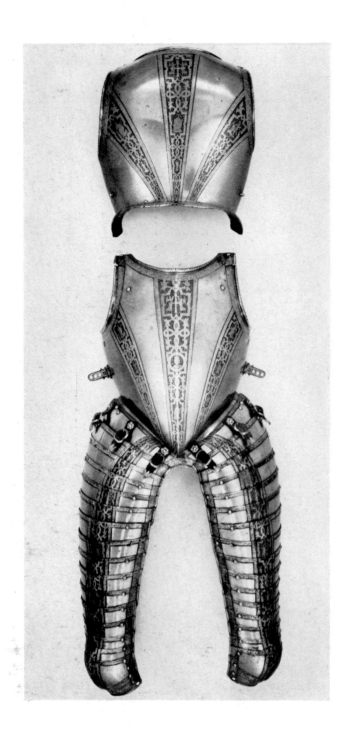

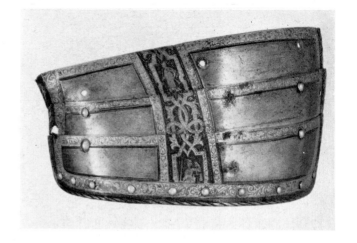

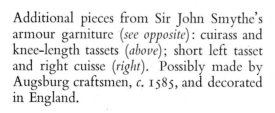

Additional pieces from Sir John Smythe's
armour garniture (*see opposite*): cuirass and
knee-length tassets (*above*); short left tasset
and right cuisse (*right*). Possibly made by
Augsburg craftsmen, *c.* 1585, and decorated
in England.

PLATE XLVIII

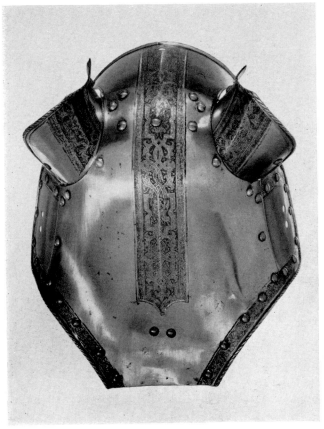

Armour (II. 84) of Sir John Smythe (1531–1607), with detail of decoration on breast; (*below*) half-chanfron (VI. 51). Possibly made by Augsburg craftsmen, *c.* 1585, and decorated in England. (*See also opposite and* Plates XCVIII, XCIX, CLV.)

PLATE XLIX

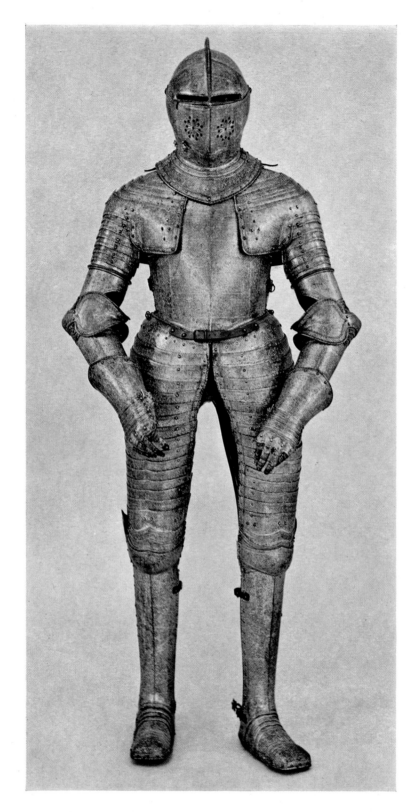

Engraved and gilt armour (II. 91) of King Charles I (1600–1649);
French or English, *c.* 1625. (*See also* Plates LI, CXLIX.)

PLATE L

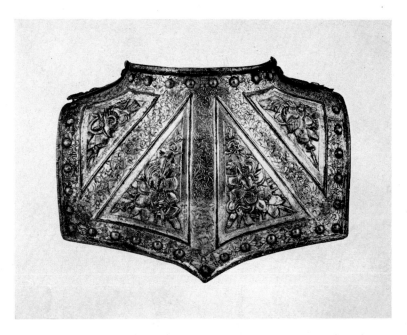

Gorget rear plate, embossed, engraved and silvered, associated with armour (II. 92) of Prince Charles, later Charles II (*see* Plate LXVI); English, *c.* 1635.

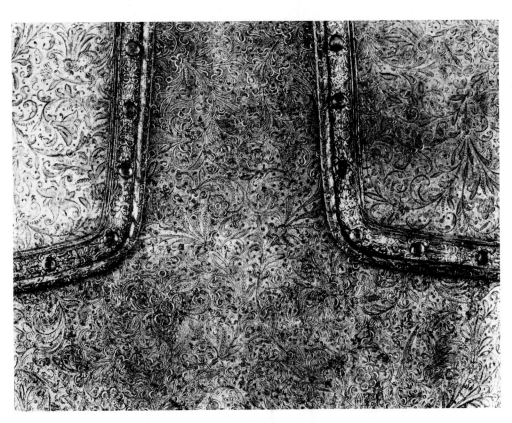

Detail of engraved and gilt decoration on back of armour (II. 91) of Charles I (*see opposite*); French or English, *c.* 1625.

PLATE LI

E*

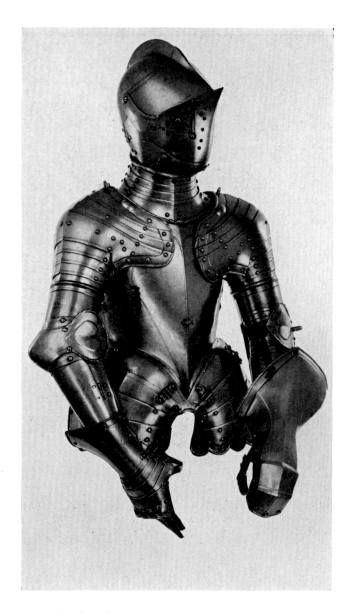

Tilt armour (II. 80); made in Royal Work-shops at Greenwich, *c.* 1615. One of five similar armours.

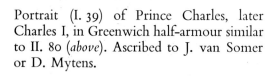

Portrait (I. 39) of Prince Charles, later Charles I, in Greenwich half-armour similar to II. 80 (*above*). Ascribed to J. van Somer or D. Mytens.

Plate LII

Pikeman's pot helmet and target *en suite* with
armour (II. 90); for chanfron *see* Plate CXLIX.

Armour (II. 90) of Prince Charles (born 1630), later Charles II, decorated
with gilt bands of engraving; French or English, *c.* 1645.

PLATE LIII

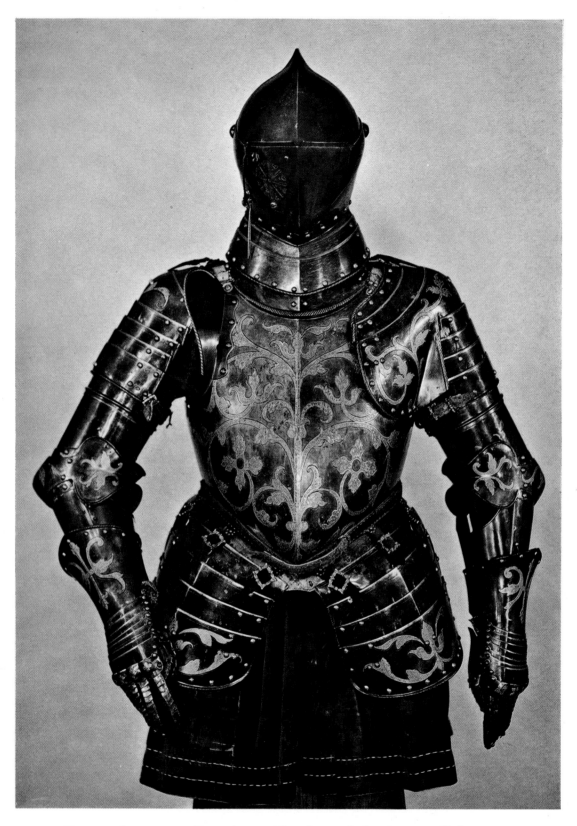

Foot-combat armour (II. 186), one of twelve made by Anton Peffenhauser
of Augsburg in 1591 for a Christmas present from the Electress Sophia to
Christian I of Saxony (1560-1591); but he died in September. From the
Royal Armoury at Dresden. Front view. (*See also* Plate CI.)

PLATE LIV

Augsburg foot-combat armour, blued and gilt (*see opposite*).   Back view.

PLATE LV

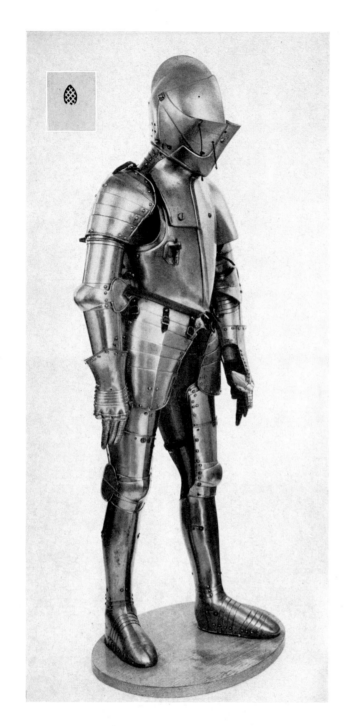

German tilt armours.

(II. 184); Augsburg, *c.* 1590–1600.   (II. 185); Augsburg, *c.* 1590–1600.

PLATE LVI

German tilt armours.

(II. 170); Saxon, *c.* 1580–90.   (II. 74); Augsburg, *c.* 1580–90.

PLATE LVII

Portrait (I. 49) of Matthias, Archduke of Austria (1557–1619), aged 21, in North Italian etched and gilt armour. Dated 1577 and with monogram AB.

PLATE LVIII

Corselet (II. 47), with etched bands, etc.; North Italian, *c.* 1570.

Corselet (II. 42; IV. 72); North Italian, *c.* 1570.

PLATE LIX

Parts of half armour (II. 25), with etched bands; (*left*) detail of decoration on breast; Italian, *c.* 1560.

Right: Detail of decoration on breast of armour (II. 146) *opposite.*

PLATE LX

Below: Field and tilt armour (II. 146), with etched and gilt bands; Italian, *c.* 1580, gauntlets associated. By tradition from ducal armoury at Lucca.

Above: Field and tilt armour (II. 180), with etched and gilt bands; French or Italian, *c.* 1570, right gauntlet associated.

PLATE LXI

Three-quarter armour (II. 164); Flemish or Italian, *c.* 1550. From Armoury of the Earls of Pembroke at Wilton House.

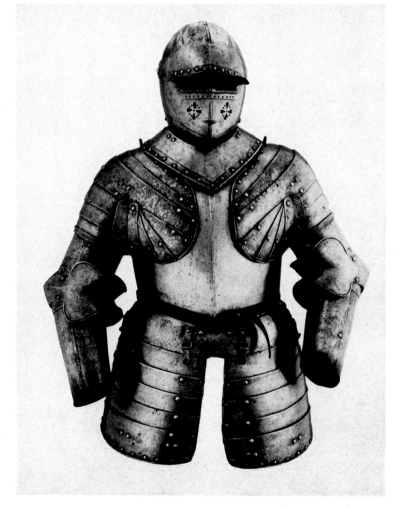

Half armour (II. 141); probably Swiss, *c.* 1620.

PLATE LXII

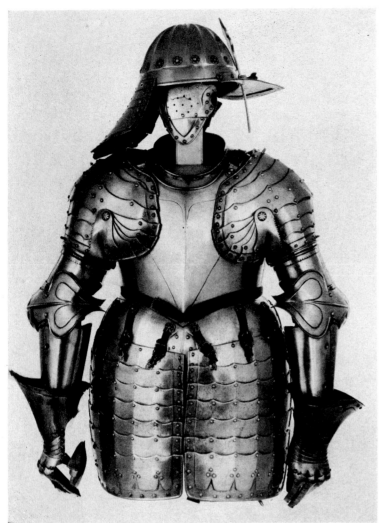

Half armour (II. 162); Swiss, c. 1630–40.

Composite siege armour (II. 138); English,
mid 17th century.

PLATE LXIII

Left: Pikeman's armour; English, early 17th century. Lent by Trustees of Dymoke Estates.

Right: Pikeman's armour (II. 112); English, early 17th century.

PLATE LXIV

Left: Pikeman's armour (II. 117); English, *c.* 1630–40.

Right: Pikeman's armour (II. 139; III. 1167), with P (for Pembroke) on tassets; English, early 17th century. From Armoury of the Earls of Pembroke at Wilton House.

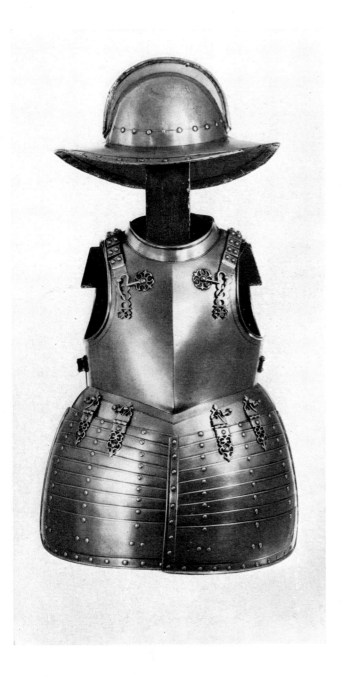

PLATE LXV

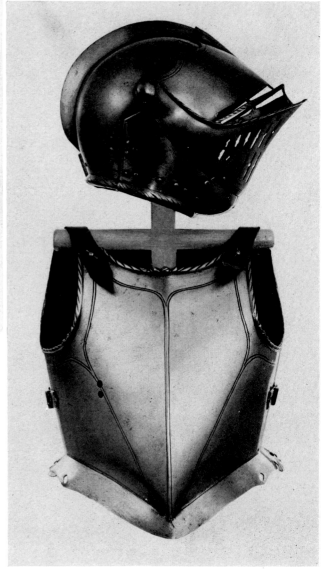

Pot helmet and cuirass (II. 92) of Prince Charles, later Charles II, with engraved and silvered surface; English *c.* 1635.

Close helmet and cuirass (II. 124) for a boy aged about 8 years; made *c.* 1600 in Royal Workshops at Greenwich.

PLATE LXVI

Harquebus armour (II. 123) of King James II (1633–1701), with royal arms and initials IR (Iacobus Rex) on face-guard of helmet; made by Richard Hoden of London, 1686. Shown here over buff coat.

PLATE LXVII

F

Model armour (II. 126), 37 ins. tall; probably
English, *c.* 1600.

Three-quarter armour (II. 163), for boy aged
about eight; probably German, *c.* 1630.

PLATE LXVIII

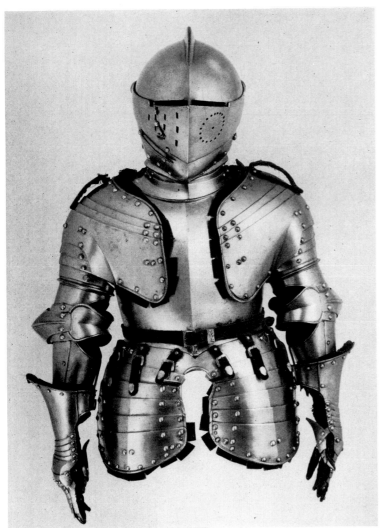

Half armour (II. 161), for boy aged about ten; probably made in Augsburg, c. 1610. From Armoury of the Duke of Saxe-Altenburg.

Half armour (II. 160), for boy aged about eight; probably made in Augsburg, c. 1610. From Armoury of the Duke of Saxe-Altenburg.

PLATE LXIX

F*

Cuirassier armour (II. 140); probably
German, *c.* 1630.

Toy cuirassier armour (II. 176), 19½ ins.
high; German or Flemish, *c.* 1630.

Plate LXX

Portrait (I. 41) of Louis XIII of France (1601–43) crowned by Victory; from series commissioned by Marie de Medici for Palais du Luxembourg. Painted by Rubens' assistants Justus van Egmont and Simon de Vos.

PLATE LXXI

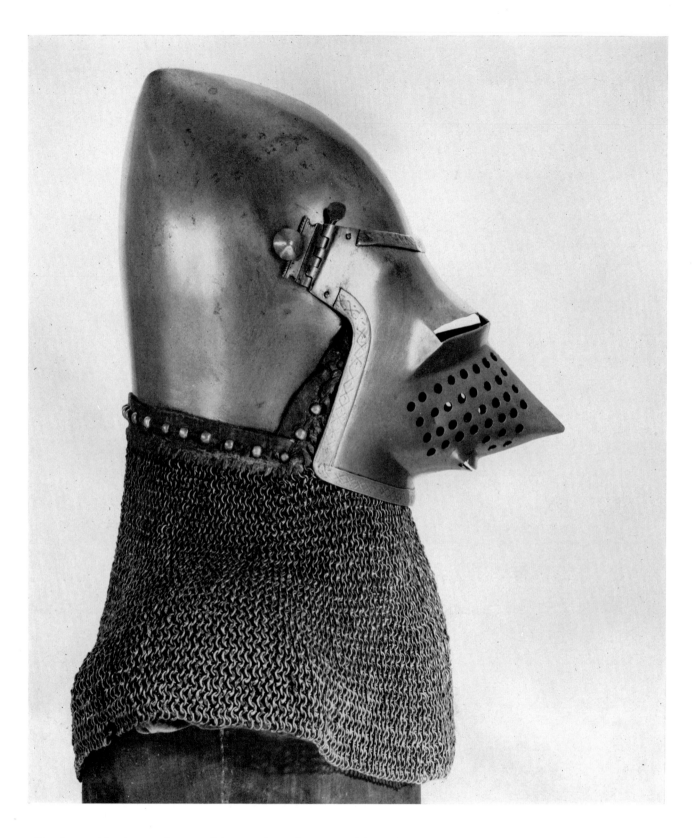

Bascinet with visor and aventail (IV. 470), with engraved brass borders to visor; North Italian, *c.* 1380–1400. From Armoury at Churburg.

PLATE LXXII

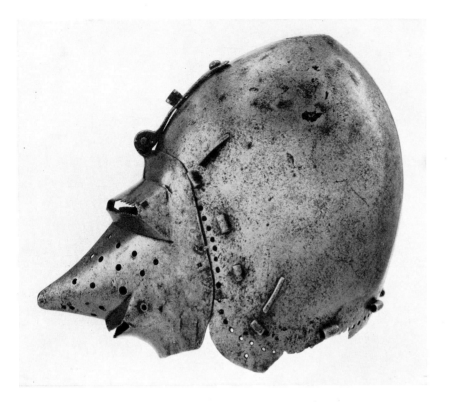

Bascinet with visor (IV. 467); visor of the *Klappvisier* type; German, c. 1370–80.

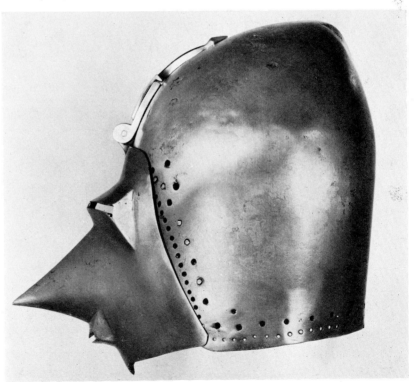

Bascinet with visor (IV. 6); probably German, c. 1380, visor hinge and fastening restored.

PLATE LXXIII

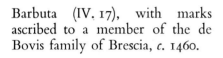

Barbuta (IV. 17), with marks ascribed to a member of the de Bovis family of Brescia, *c.* 1460.

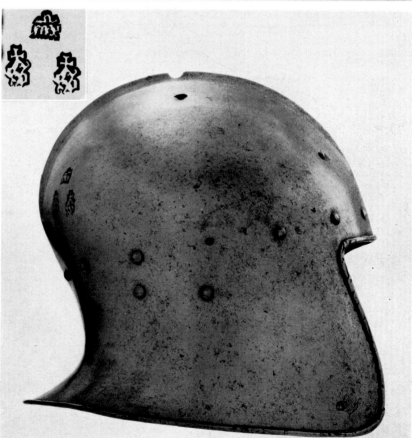

Barbuta (IV. 7), with unidentified marks; Italian, mid 15th century.

PLATE LXXIV

Barbuta (IV. 18), with maker's marks; North Italian, *c.* 1470.

Sallet (IV. 8), with maker's indeterminate marks; North Italian, *c.* 1470–80; visor missing.

PLATE LXXV

Sallet, now on armour II. 168 (*see* Plate VII); North Italian (Milanese), *c.* 1460. From Armoury at Churburg.

PLATE LXXVI

Sallet (IV. 424), with mark attributed to Domenico Negroli of Milan, *c*. 1470–80. From Rhodes.

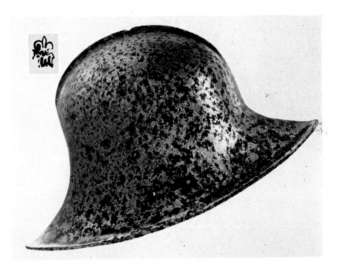

Sallet (IV. 453), with 'castle' mark; North Italian, *c*. 1480–90, neck lames restored.

Kettle hat (IV. 425), with unidentified maker's mark; N. Italian, probably Milanese, *c*. 1480. From Rhodes.

Sallet (IV. 20), with red velvet cover and gilt copper mounts; Italian, *c*. 1480.

PLATE LXXVII

Cabacete (IV. 500), stamped with unidentified maker's mark; Spanish, or Italian for Spanish market, late 15th century.

Morion (IV. 490), with two unidentified maker's marks; probably Italian, c. 1520–30.

Sallet (IV. 9), stamped with mark of Calatayud or *Castejón de las armas* (Zaragoza); Spanish, late 15th century.

PLATE LXXVIII

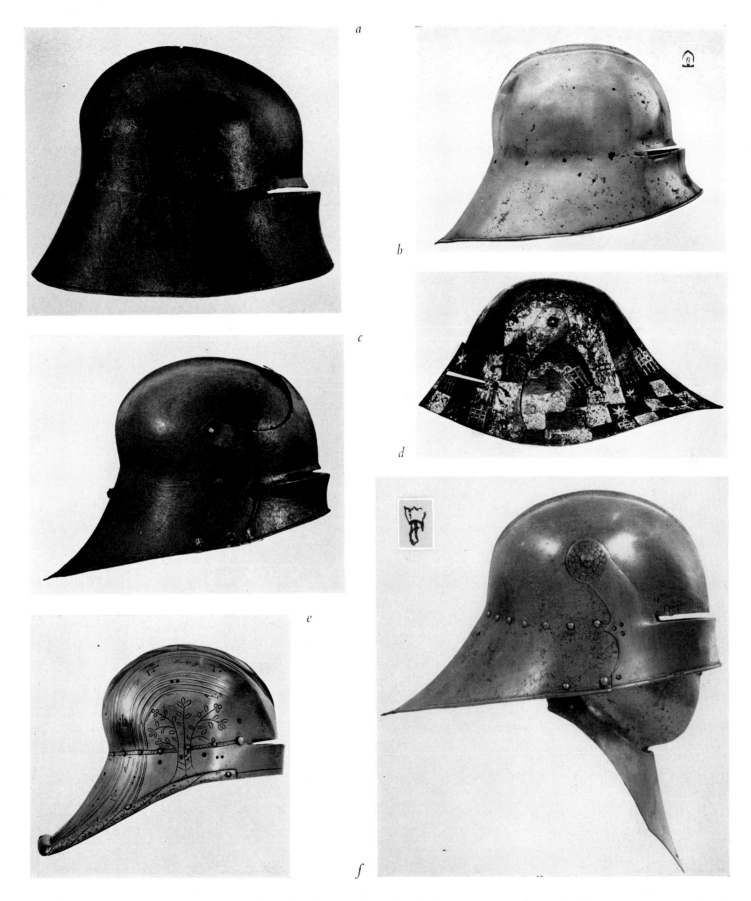

Sallets. *a:* (IV. 429); German, *c.* 1450. From Rhodes. *b:* From (II. 3) (*see* Plate II); with mark of Jörg Treytz of Innsbruck, *c.* 1470–80. *c:* (IV. 427); German, *c.* 1480. From Rhodes. *d:* (IV. 12); for light horseman; surface painted with heraldic charges; German, *c.* 1490. *e: Rennhut* (IV. 16) for form of joust called *Rennen;* German, *c.* 1510–20. *f:* (IV. 499) with bevor (III. 1321); former with unidentified maker's mark; German, *c.* 1480; bevor from Armoury at Churburg.

PLATE LXXIX

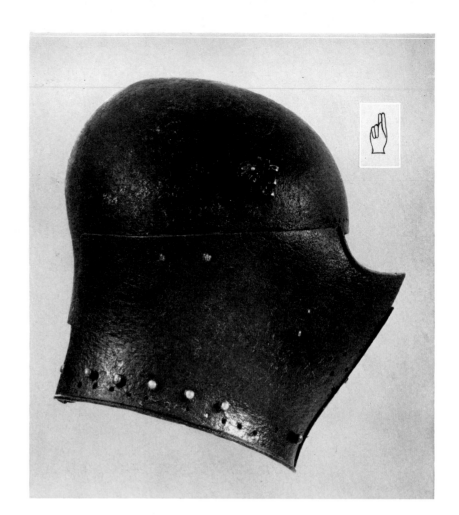

Armet (IV. 430), with maker's mark (? Benedetto da Molteno); North Italian, *c.* 1440; the visor missing. From Rhodes.

Armet (IV. 468), with maker's mark of Hans Rabeiler of Innsbruck, *c.* 1500.

PLATE LXXX

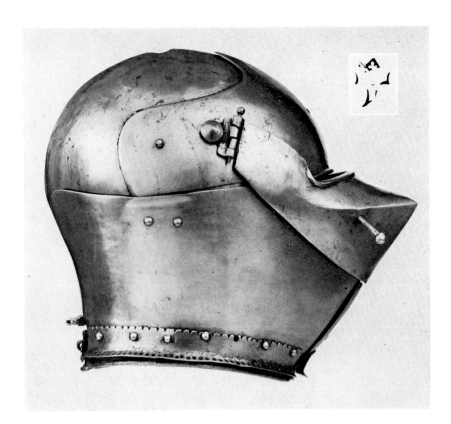

Armet (IV. 498), stamped twice with unidentified maker's mark; North Italian (Milanese), *c.* 1450. From Armoury at Churburg.

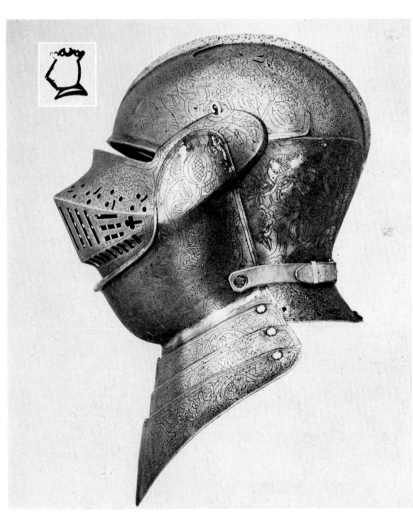

Armet of engraved and silvered armour (II. 5) of King Henry VIII, *c.* 1514. (*See* Plates I, XIV, XV.)

PLATE LXXXI

Grotesque helmet (IV. 22), only surviving piece from the armour presented to King Henry VIII by the Emperor Maximilian I; made by Conrad Seusenhofer, Innsbruck, 1511–14.

PLATE LXXXII

Tilt helm (IV. 1), with two maker's marks on skull; probably Flemish, *c.* 1510.

PLATE LXXXIII

G

Tilt helmet (IV. 502), for a type of joust known as *Welchgestech;* probably Augsburg, *c.* 1490–1500. From Imperial Armoury, Vienna.

PLATE LXXXIV

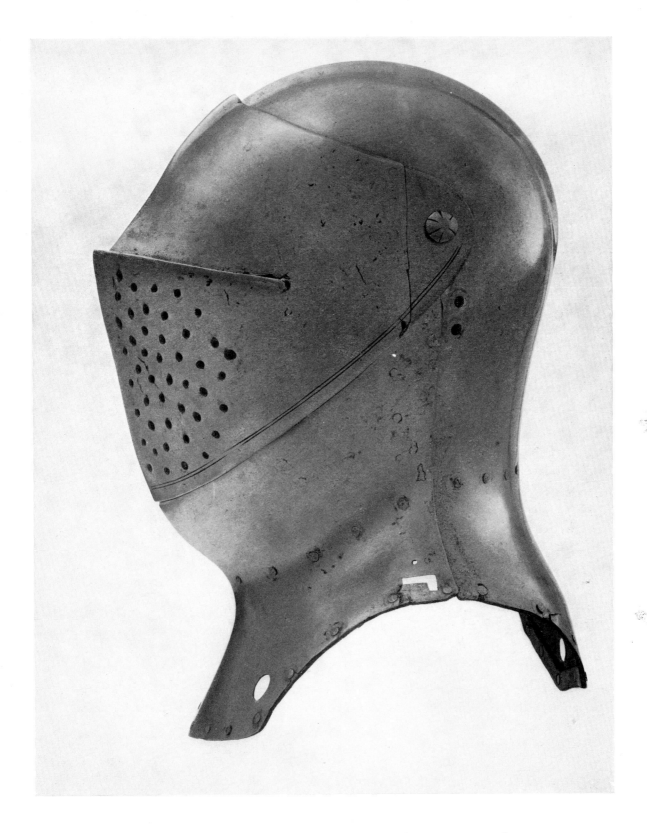

Great bascinet (IV. 2); possibly made in Royal Workshops at Greenwich, *c.* 1515.

PLATE LXXXV

G*

Tilt helm (IV. 411), known as the 'Brocas' helm; English ?, c. 1490.

Plate LXXXVI

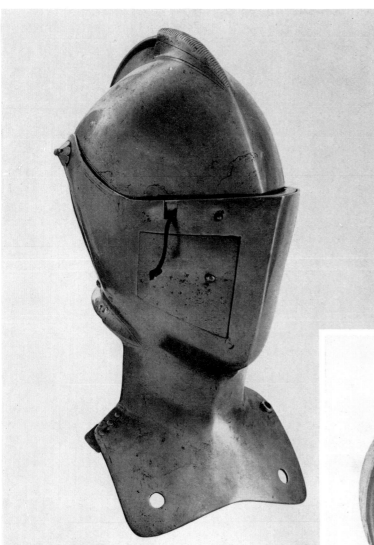

Tilt helmet (IV. 39); German, *c.* 1570.

Close helmet, from foot-combat armour (II. 6) of King Henry VIII (*see* Plates XII, XIII); Greenwich, *c.*1515-20.

PLATE LXXXVII

Close helmet (IV. 413); Italian or Flemish, *c.* 1520.

PLATE LXXXVIII

(IV. 26); *c.* 1515.

(IV. 36); *c.* 1540.

(IV. 521); *c.* 1530.

(IV. 24); *c.* 1515.

Close helmets; English or Flemish, first half of 16th century.

Plate LXXXIX

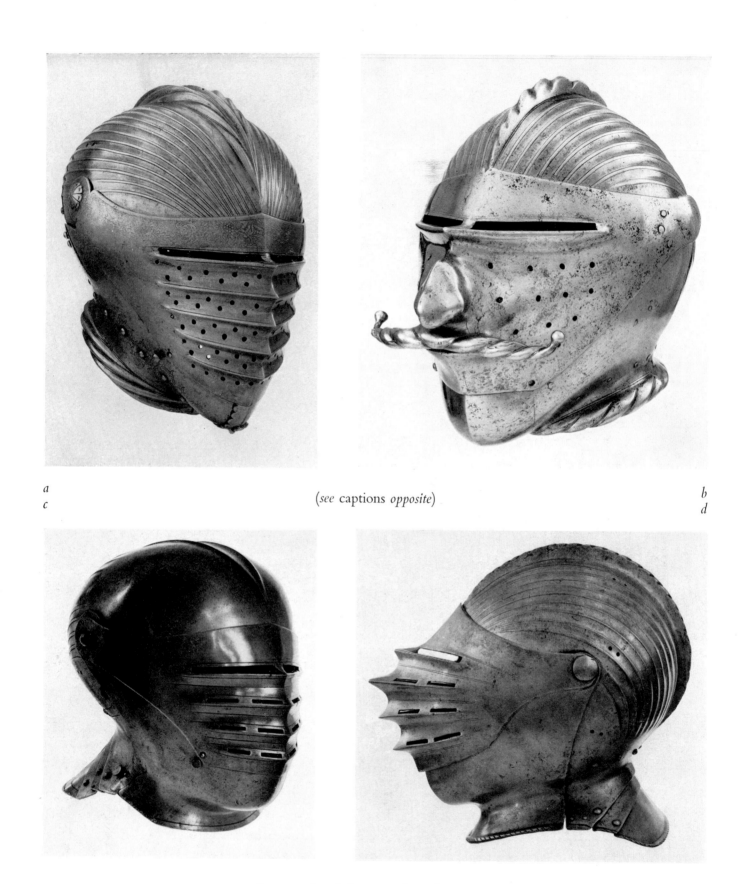

(*see* captions *opposite*)

a
c

b
d

German close helmets, early 16th century.

PLATE XC

From armour (II. 2); with Nuremberg
mark, *c.* 1520. (*see* Plate V.)

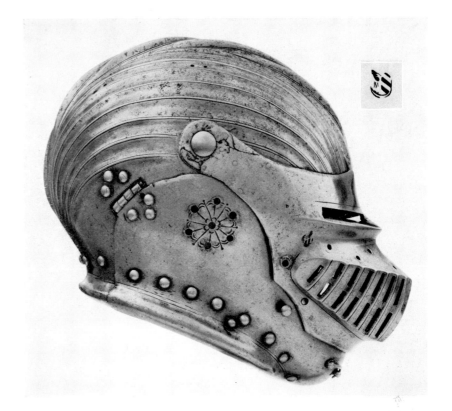

a: (IV. 412), etched and gilt;
          probably Innsbruck, *c.* 1510–15.

b: (IV. 29), with grotesque visor; *c.* 1520.

c: From armour (II. 14), with fluted comb;
          c. 1515.

d: (IV. 472), with sharply indented visor;
          c. 1520.

(IV. 471); probably Nuremberg, *c.* 1535.

German close helmets, first half of 16th century.

PLATE XCI

(IV. 33), with wings; German, *c.* 1530.

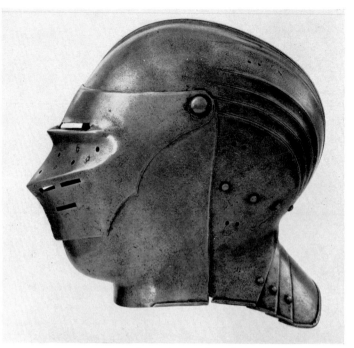

From armour (II. 12); Innsbruck, *c.* 1510.

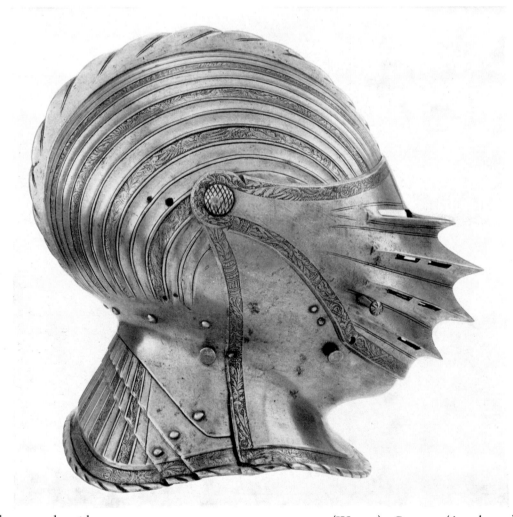

Close helmets, early 16th century.

(IV. 501); German (Augsburg?), *c.* 1520.

PLATE XCII

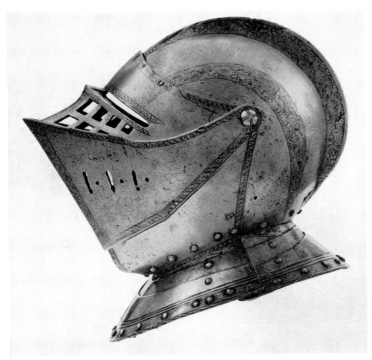

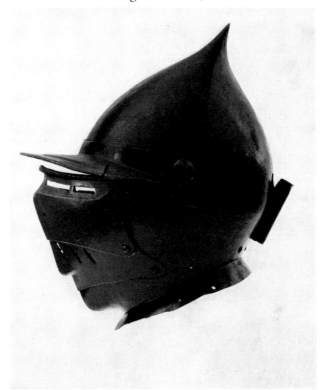

(IV. 164), with falling buffe of two lames; with Nuremberg mark, *c.* 1560.

(IV. 476); in style associated with Brunswick, *c.* 1560.

(IV. 505), with reinforcing pate plate; probably Innsbruck, *c.* 1550.

Close helmets, mid to late 16th century.

(IV. 474); perhaps French, *c.* 1590.

PLATE XCIII

Field close helmet (IV. 41); made in Royal Workshops at Greenwich, *c.* 1570.

Tilt close helmet, from armour (II. 81) of Robert Dudley, K.G., Earl of Leicester (*see* Plates XLIV, XLV); made in Royal Workshops at Greenwich, *c.* 1575.

PLATE XCIV

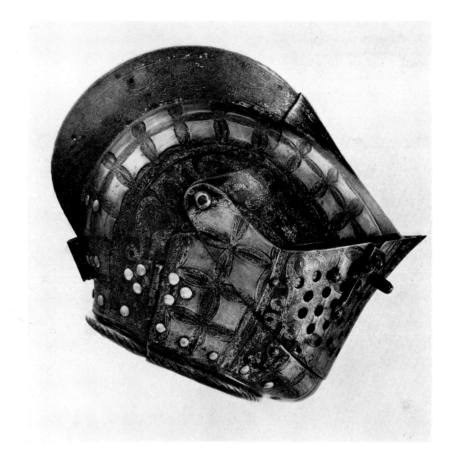

Tilt close helmet (IV. 43) of Sir Henry Lee, K.G., Master of the Armouries 1578–1610; made in Royal Workshops at Greenwich, *c.* 1580.

Tilt close helmet, from armour (II. 78); made in Royal Workshops at Greenwich, *c.* 1590.

PLATE XCV

Close helmet, from armour (II. 89), embossed with lion's mask and damascened with gold (*see* Plate XXVI); French or Italian, *c.* 1540–50.

PLATE XCVI

Burgonet (IV. 154), embossed with patterns of birds and fruit and with applied decorative plaques and borders of copper gilt; German, last quarter of 16th century.

PLATE XCVII

Burgonet with falling buffe, etched and gilt, from armour (II. 84) of Sir John Smythe (*see* Plate XLIX). Possibly made by Augsburg craftsmen, *c.* 1585.

PLATE XCVIII

Morion, etched and gilt, from armour of Sir John Smythe (*see opposite*).

PLATE XCIX

H

a

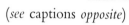

(*see* captions *opposite*)

b

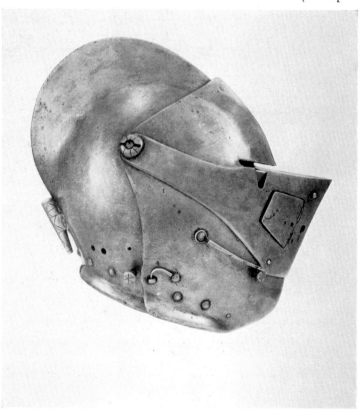

c

d

Close helmets, mid to late 16th century.

PLATE C

From armour (II. 186) for the foot combat (*see* Plate LIV); Augsburg, 1591.

a : (IV. 51); English or Flemish, *c.* 1560.

b : (IV. 416); probably Augsburg, *c.* 1580.

c : (IV. 414); probably Augsburg, *c.* 1580.

d : From armour (II. 33); German *c.* 1575.

From armour (II. 182), with etched and gilt bands; North Italian, *c.* 1580.

Close helmets, late 16th century.

PLATE CI

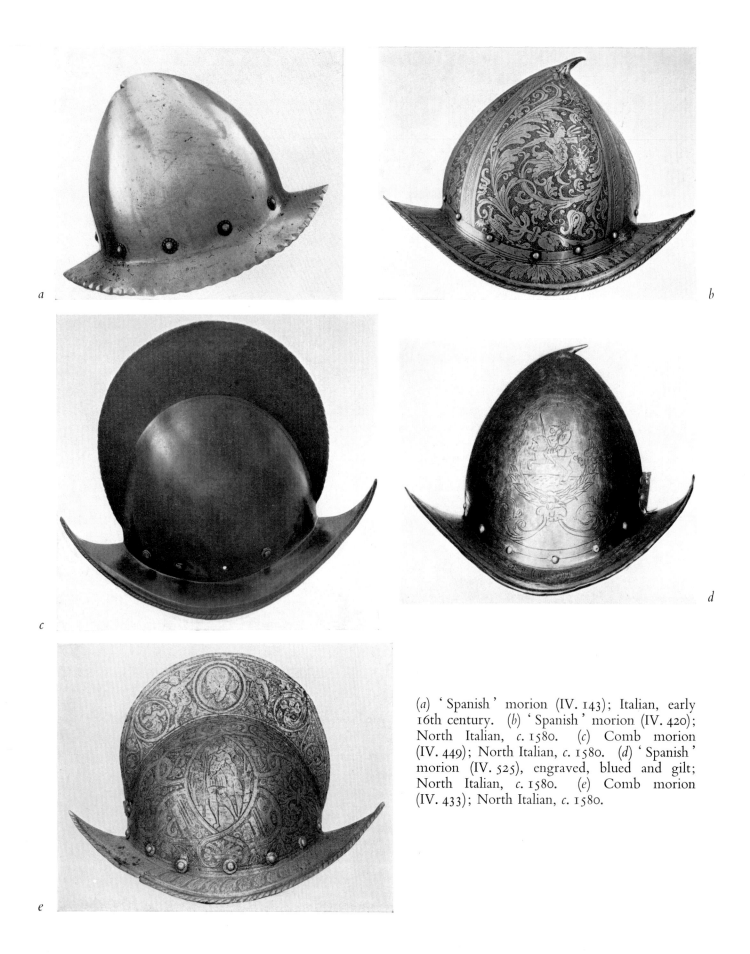

a

b

c

d

(*a*) 'Spanish' morion (IV. 143); Italian, early 16th century. (*b*) 'Spanish' morion (IV. 420); North Italian, *c.* 1580. (*c*) Comb morion (IV. 449); North Italian, *c.* 1580. (*d*) 'Spanish' morion (IV. 525), engraved, blued and gilt; North Italian, *c.* 1580. (*e*) Comb morion (IV. 433); North Italian, *c.* 1580.

e

PLATE CII

a

b

c

d

(*a*) 'Spanish' morion (IV. 526); North Italian, *c.* 1600. (*b*) 'Spanish' morion (IV. 144); North Italian, late 16th century. (*c*) Pot helmet (IV. 503); German or Flemish, *c.* 1630. (*d*) Pot helmet (IV. 518), heavy for siege wear; German, *c.* 1640. (*e*) Pot helmet (IV. 512); Polish, *c.* 1640.

e

PLATE CIII

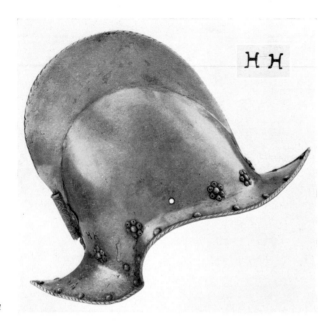

a

c

b

d

a : (IV. 417), stamped with maker's initials HH
(Hans Hörburger the elder); Innsbruck, *c.* 1570.
b : (IV. 529); English, Greenwich, *c.* 1575.
c : (IV. 443); Italian, *c.* 1550.
d : (IV. 350); English, Greenwich, late 16th century.
e : (IV. 523), rough from hammer, with original blue-
black surface; probably Augsburg, *c.* 1550–60.

Burgonets, 16th century.

e

PLATE CIV

a : Trooper's pot (IV. 159); North
European, mid 17th century.
b : 'Spider' (IV. 211); French (?), late
17th century.
c : Trooper's pot (IV. 174); English,
mid 17th century.
d : Zischägge (IV. 519); East European,
late 17th century.
e : Officer's pot (IV. 165); German or
Flemish, c. 1630.

d

a

e

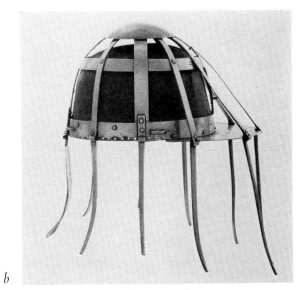

b

f

f : Trooper's pot (IV. 185); English,
mid 17th century.

c

Open helmets etc., 17th century.

PLATE CV

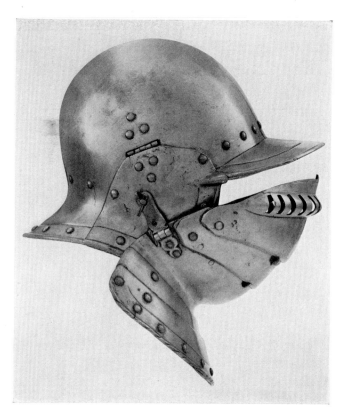

Left: Burgonet (IV. 166); English, Greenwich, second half of 16th century.
Right: Burgonet (IV. 156), with falling buffe; English, Greenwich, *c.* 1570.

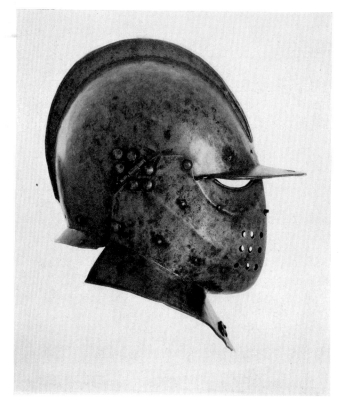

Left: Close helmet (IV. 522), with double visor; English, early 17th century.
Right: Burgonet (IV. 485); probably Flemish, *c.* 1630. From Wilton House.

PLATE CVI

Left: Close helmet (IV. 506), heavy for siege wear; English, *c.* 1640.
Right: Cuirassier helmet (IV. 516); probably German, *c.* 1630.

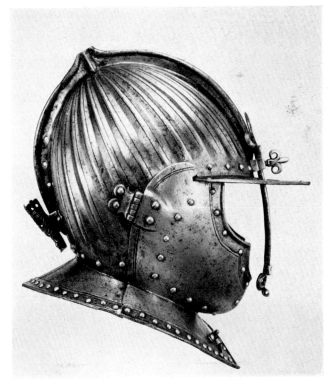

Left: Close helmet (IV. 48), *Todenkopf* or *Savoyard* type; Italian, *c.* 1620.
Right: Burgonet (IV. 524), with adjustable nasal; French, *c.* 1630.

PLATE CVII

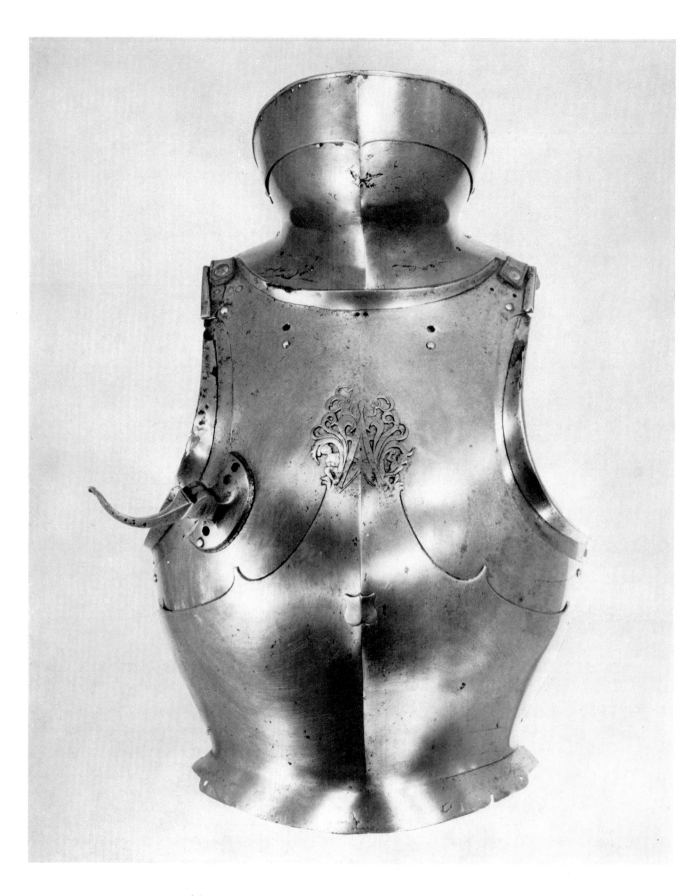

Bevor and breastplate (III. 1227–8); apex of plackart (lower breast) pierced
and engraved with human figures, foliage and unicorn; German, *c.* 1480.

PLATE CVIII

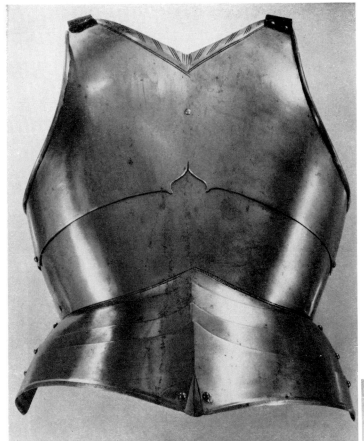

Backplate (III. 1284); probably Innsbruck, *c.* 1480. From Armoury at Churburg.

Breastplate (III. 1282), with Milanese marks; Italian, *c.* 1470. From Armoury at Churburg.

PLATE CIX

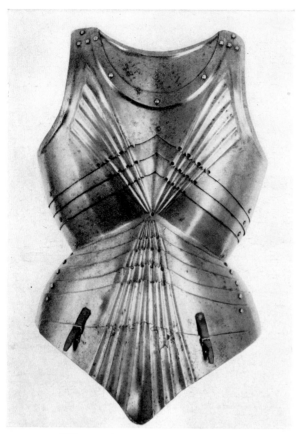

(III. 1287); German, *c.* 1480–90.

a
b

(III. 1325), with marks (*a*) unidentified, (*b*) of Augsburg; *c.* 1480.

(III. 71); probably Flemish, *c.* 1500.

(III. 1092); probably German, *c.* 1480, lower plates missing. From Rhodes.

Cuirass (*below left*) and backplates, late 15th century.

PLATE CX

(III. 1293–4), with mark of Caspar Rieder of Innsbruck; *c.* 1500.

(III. 1093), with Milanese maker's mark;
c. 1470, lower plates missing. From Rhodes.

(III. 1283); German, *c.* 1480.

Cuirass (*above*), breast and backplates, late 15th century.

PLATE CXI

(III. 1246), engraved HILF MIR MARIA (*breastplate*) HILF RITER SANT IORG (*backplate*); Innsbruck, *c.* 1510.

Below left: (III. 85), plain; North Italian, *c.* 1510.

(III. 1087), of pronounced form, with heavily roped borders; North Italian, *c.* 1520. From Rhodes.

Cuirass (*above*) and breastplates, early 16th century.

PLATE CXII

(III. 1086); Italian, *c.* 1515. From Rhodes.

Below right: From armour (II. 11), embossed and etched; German, *c.* 1530.

(III. 75); German, *c.* 1515.

(III. 1090); Italian, *c.* 1500. From Rhodes.

Breastplates and cuirass (*below right*), early 16th century.

PLATE CXIII

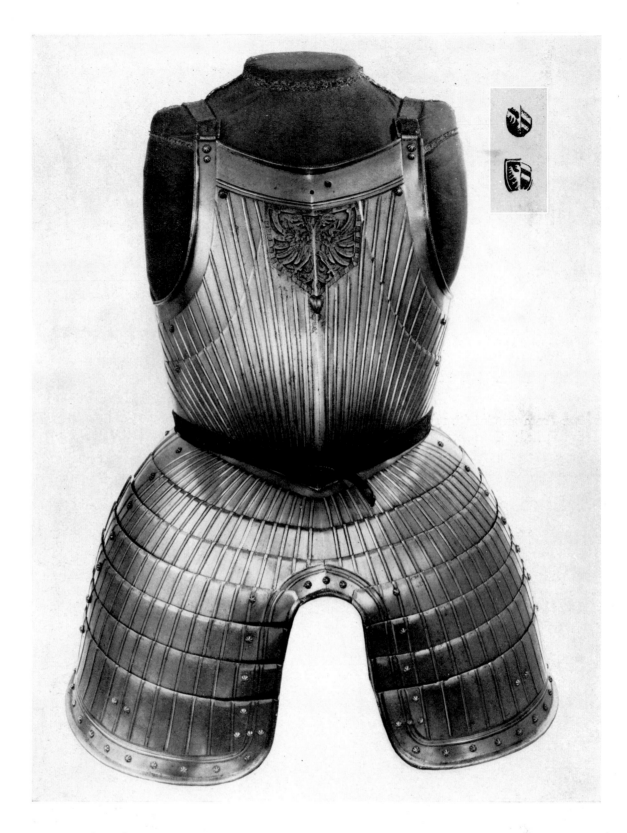

Cuirass (III. 1288–9), with radiating ridges and pierced and engraved enrichment, on breast double-headed eagle of the Empire, on back sea-lion badge of Imhof (?) of Nuremberg (*see opposite*); with Nuremberg marks and dated 1612.

PLATE CXIV

Sea-lion badge (*see opposite*).

(II. 16); Italian, *c.* 1560.

(II. 18); Italian, *c.* 1560.

Animes (laminated cuirasses).

(III. 94–5); East European, *c.* 1600.

PLATE CXV

1

(III. 1297); South German, *c.* 1560.

(III. 1338), etched with badges associated with
Rocco Guerrini, Count of Lynar (1525–96);
German, *c.* 1560.

(III. 117), with etched and gilt bands;
Italian, *c.* 1610.

Breastplates and backplate, 16th and 17th century.

(III. 118); probably French, *c.* 1570.

(III. 1218); Flemish, *c.* 1590.

(III. 104); North German, *c.* 1570.

(III. 99); North Italian, *c.* 1580.

Breastplates and 'waistcoat' cuirass, late 16th century.

PLATE CXVII

(III. 1251), with gorget, with narrow bands recessed and gilt; probably French, c. 1530.

Cuirass (*above*) and backplates.

Below left: (III. 100); North Italian, c. 1570.
Below right: (III. 1329); North Italian, c. 1600.

PLATE CXVIII

Above left: (III. 1058), with engraved badge of
stag and motto SPERO IN DIO; Italian, *c.* 1550.
Above right: (III. 1328); North Italian, *c.* 1600.

Breastplates and tilt cuirass (*below*).

(III. 1336); Flemish or Italian, early 16th century.

PLATE CXIX

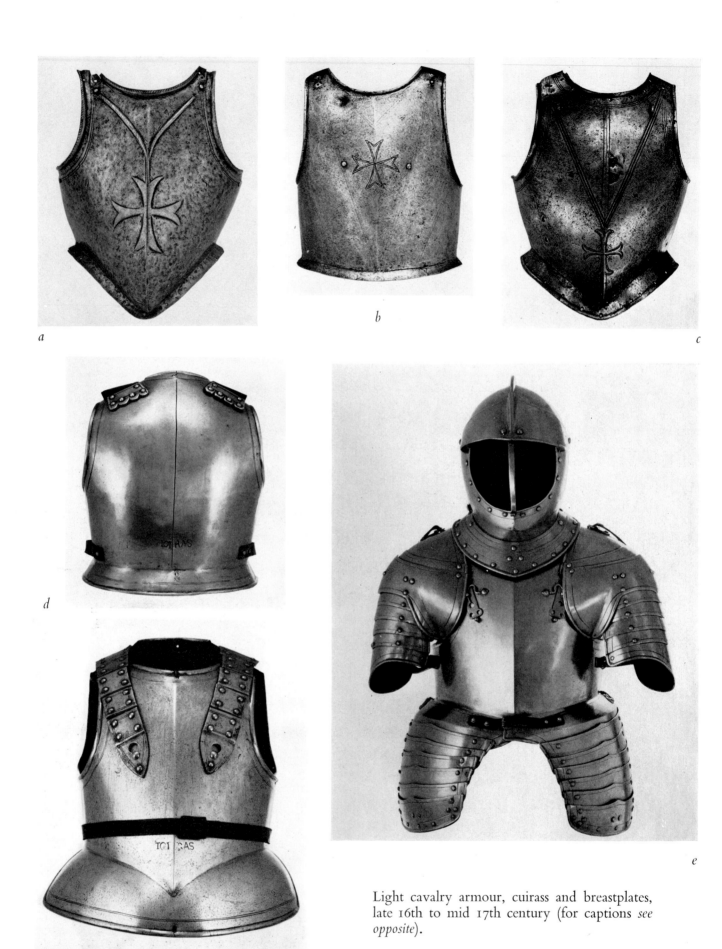

a

b

c

d

Light cavalry armour, cuirass and breastplates, late 16th to mid 17th century (for captions *see opposite*).

e

Plate CXX

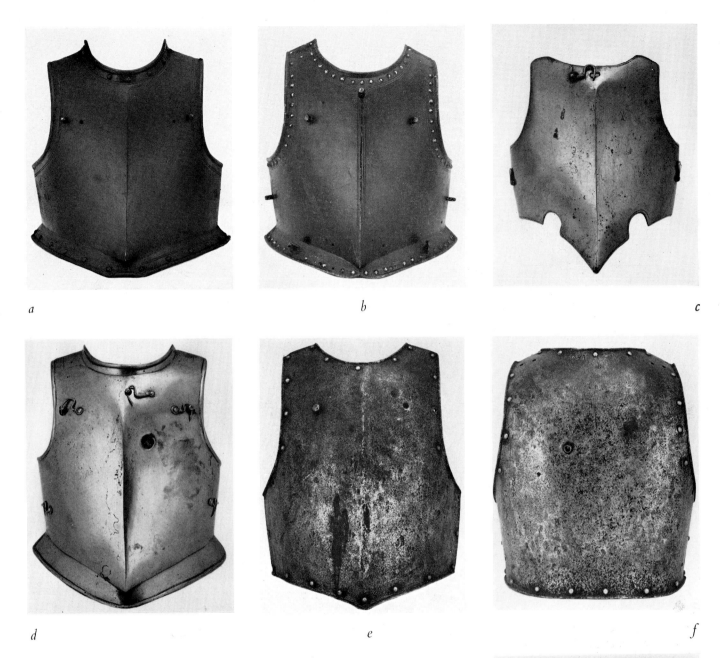

a   b   c

d   e   f

Breastplates, backplate, etc., 17th century.   g

(*a*) (III. 1342), for trooper; English, *c.* 1640.   (*b*) (III. 1341), for cuirassier; probably English, *c.* 1630.   (*c*) (III. 400), plackart (reinforcing breast), for cuirassier; English, *c.* 1620.   (*d*) (III. 148), with plackart, for trooper; by Richard Hoden of London, *c.* 1675.   (*e*) (III. 1031), for trooper; English, *c.* 1700.   (*f*) (III. 1027), for trooper; English, *c.* 1700.   (*g*) (III. 429), for trooper; *c.* 1640, faced with brass *c.* 1820 for issue to Royal Horse Guards.

(*Opposite*) (*a*) (III. 905), embossed with cross moline; Italian, *c.* 1580. (*b*) (III. 127), engraved with cross moline; Italian, early 17th century. (*c*) (III. 1327), engraved with cross moline; Italian, late 16th century. (*d*) (III. 250), breast and back engraved 'TOIRAS'; captured from the French under Marshal Toiras in 1627.   (*e*) (II. 108), light cavalry armour; probably English, mid 17th century.

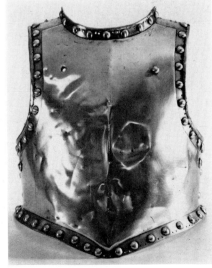

PLATE CXXI

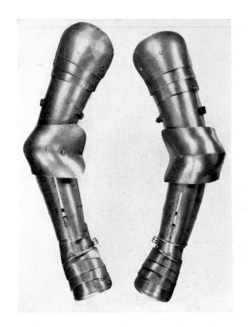

Top: (III. 1165) pair of splints; German, Nuremberg, *c.* 1500–10.

Middle left: (III. 773); probably English, *c.* 1375. Excavated in Brick Hill Lane, London.

Middle: (III. 782–3), with Landshut town mark; German, *c.* 1490.

Middle right: (III. 1214), with Milanese maker's marks; Italian, *c.* 1470.

Below left: (III. 1264) bridle gauntlet, from armour (A 880) at Vienna; Augsburg, *c.* 1570.

Below centre: (III. 792) linen glove protected by gold damascened scales, possibly from one of Charles V's armours; Italian, early 16th century.

Below right: (III. 813), embossed with flowers and tendrils; Italian, Milanese, *c.* 1540.

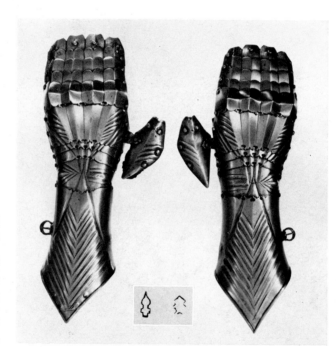

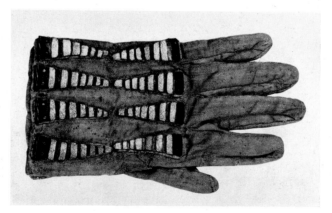

Arm defences and gauntlets, 14th–16th century.

PLATE CXXII

Composite armour: brigandine (III. 47), of small plates riveted to linen covers, probably German; *cabacete* (IV. 500), bevor (III. 1300) and gauntlets (III. 1197–8) all probably Spanish; *c.* 1470–1500.

Below left: Jack (III. 1277), of small plates sewn between quilted linen; English, *c.* 1580.

Below right: Jack (II. 27); English, *c.* 1560.

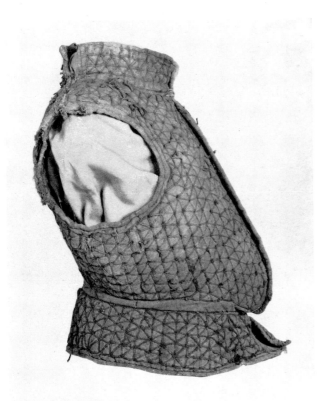

Brigandine and jacks, etc.

PLATE CXXIII

Portrait (I. 47) of Sir John Robinson, Lord Mayor of London (1662–3) and Lieutenant of the Tower of London (1660–80), by John Michael Wright (1617?–1700). Lord Mayor's collar and robe on table in foreground and White Tower in background.

PLATE CXXIV

Buff leather coats.
a: (III. 1226); probably Swedish, of the early 18th century.
b: (III. 1157), with sword belt (XIII. 119); mid 17th century.
c: (III. 1301), traditionally that of Colonel Francis Hacker, the regicide; mid 17th century.

PLATE CXXV

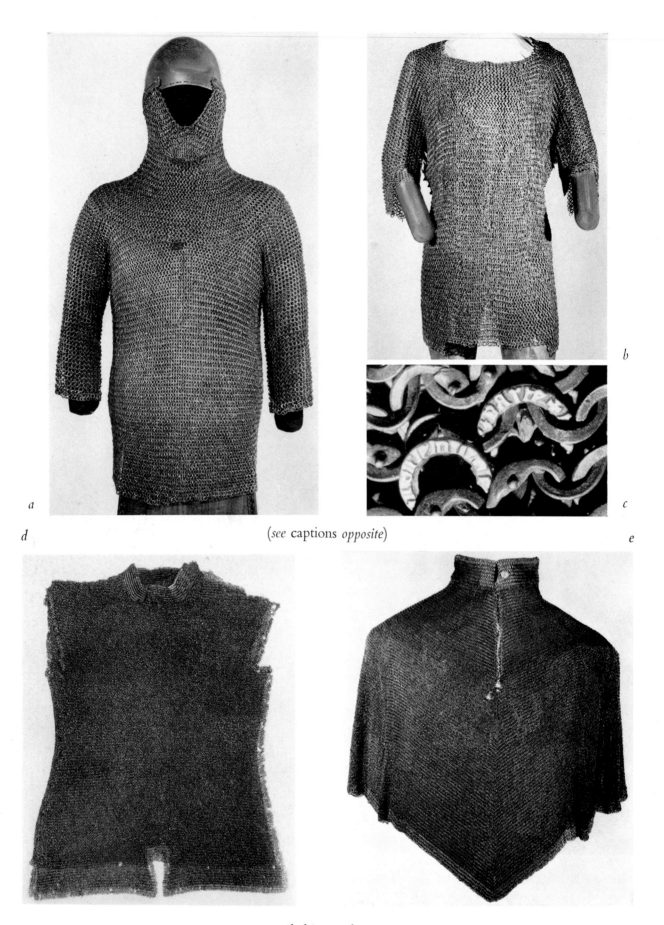

a

b

c

d

(*see* captions *opposite*)

e

Mail shirts and cape.

Plate CXXVI

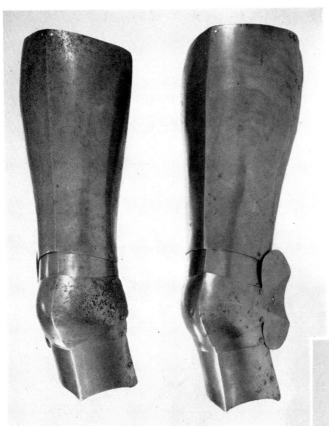

Cuisses (III. 1285–6); probably North Italian, late 14th century. From Armoury at Churburg.

Cuisses from armour (II. 1), with mark of Klaus Wagner of Innsbruck; *c.* 1480–90.

a: Mail shirt (III. 1279), by tradition that of Rudolf IV, Duke of Austria and Styria (1339–65), and aventail (III. 1280); German, 14th century (bascinet modern).

b, c: Mail shirt (III. 1320), with brass rings signed BERTOLT VOR PARTE and TO ISRENLOEN (Bertolt vor Parte of Iserlohn, maker); German, *c.* 1400.

d: Sleeveless mail shirt (III. 9), of small rings, with brass borders; probably German, mid 16th century.

e: Mail cape ('bishop's mantle') (III. 1252); German, early 16th century.

PLATE CXXVII

Parts of parade armour (II. 10), puffed and slashed and decorated with etched and gilt designs to simulate brocade, all in emulation of the contemporary civilian costume; German, *c.* 1520.

Gorget.

Waistplate and tassets.

PLATE CXXVIII

Arm defences.

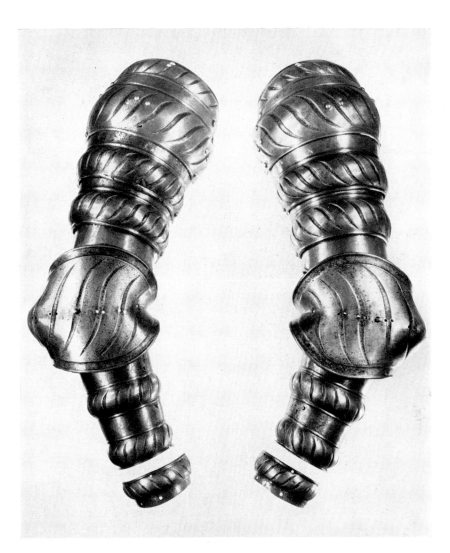

Couter.

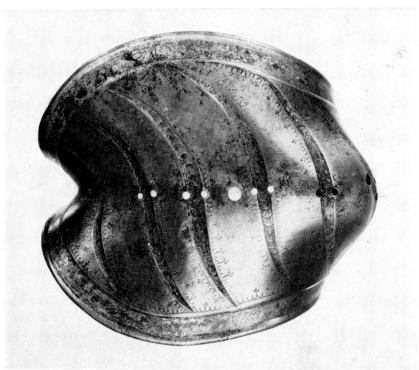

Parts of German parade armour (*see opposite*).

PLATE CXXIX

Portrait (I. 50) of Archduke Albert, Governor of the Netherlands, in
Milanese armour, parts of which are now in Brussels (Porte de Hal, SII. 83,
SIV. 1) and Cracow (Muzeum Narodowe); his palace, the 'Old Court', at
Brussels in background. Studio of Rubens.

PLATE CXXX

Pauldron and vambraces.

Chanfron (VI. 52).

Parts of parade armour (II. 85), embossed, blued, gilt
and formerly silvered; Italian, *c.* 1600.

Leg harness.

Plate CXXXI

Pauldron from armour (II. 172), *see* Plate XXIX.

Plackart (III. 1319), etched and gilt, probably from brigandine of Emperor Charles V, and (*right*) ankle defences (III. 771–2), embossed, etched and gilt, from one of his armours; all German, early 16th century.

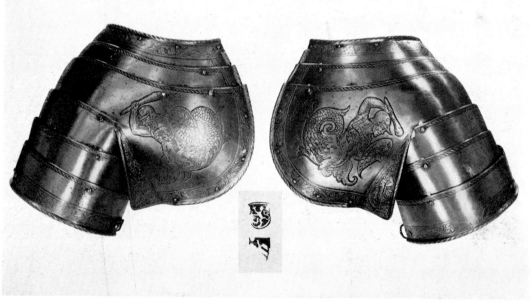

Pauldrons (III. 736–7), with mark of Kunz Lochner and (*below*) of Nuremberg; *c.* 1530.

PLATE CXXXII

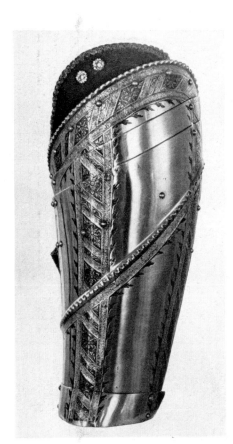

Left : Cuisse (III. 1265), with etched and gilt bands and borders; Augsburg, *c.* 1550. *Right :* Shoulder shield (III. 874), from 'Rose-leaf' garniture of the Emperor Maximilian II made probably by Franz Grosschedel of Landshut in 1571.

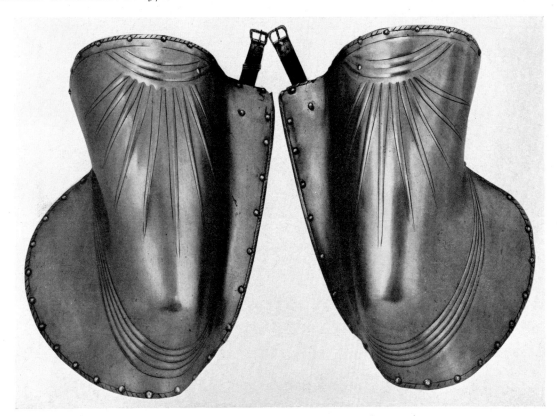

Tilt sockets (thigh defences), from *Rennzeug* (II. 167), *see* Plates VIII, IX.

PLATE CXXXIII

K

Pate plate (IV. 333), probably from a garniture of the Emperor Charles V; Augsburg, *c.* 1540.

'Wings' (IV. 520) from parade helmet, embossed and etched; German, *c.* 1530.

Jousting stirrup (VI. 348); Italian, *c.* 1570–80.

PLATE CXXXIV

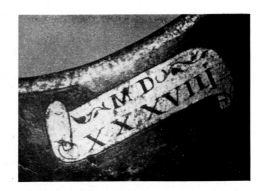

Buffe (IV. 477), embossed as male mask, russet and gilt and with two *cartellini* (*above*) inscribed PHI E FRA DE NEGROLIS F and MDXXXVIII; Milan, Negroli workshops, 1538.

Embossed poleyns (III. 850), with *goldschmelz* decoration, from an armour of the Emperor Charles V; German, early 16th century.

PLATE CXXXV

Shields (pavises) with painted decoration, 15th century.
(*a*) (V. 1), with figure of St. George, arms of Zwickau and foliage; German, *c.* 1480.
(*b*) (V. 2), with rayed monogram, arms of Zwickau and inscription; German, *c.* 1480.
(*c*) (V. 13), with figure of St. George, arms of Zwickau and inscription; German, *c.* 1480.
(*d*) (V. 7), with arms of Wimpfen; German, late 15th century.

PLATE CXXXVI

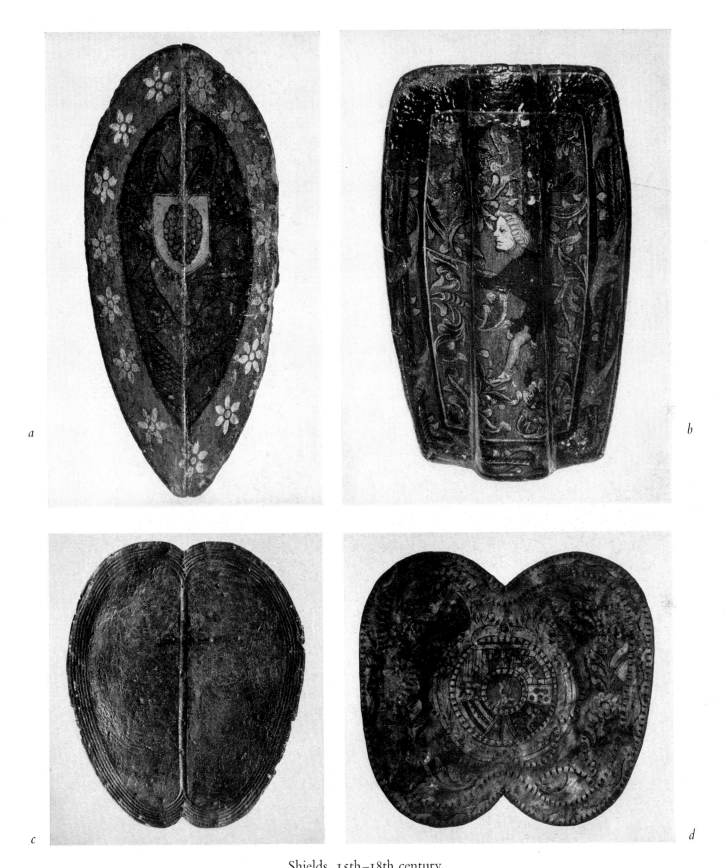

Shields, 15th–18th century.
(a) (V. 6), painted with pierced heart, scutcheon, etc., feathers and flowers; German, late 15th century.
(b) (V. 10), pavise, painted with figure of hunter and foliation; German, c. 1480.
(c) (V. 3), *adarga*, of hide, painted with strapwork arabesques; Spanish, 16th century.
(d) (V. 98), *adarga*, of hide, painted with arms of Spain and floral designs; Mexican, c. 1760.

PLATE CXXXVII

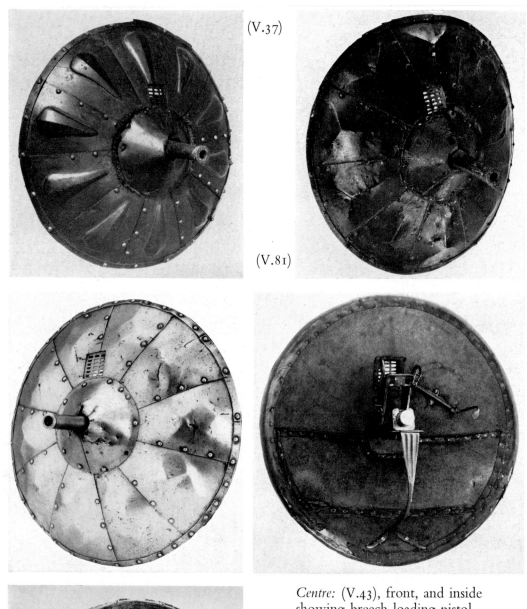

(V.37)

(V.81)

Centre: (V.43), front, and inside showing breech-loading pistol.

'Gun-shields' from Henry VIII's military stores, made probably by Giovanbattista and company of Ravenna, *c.* 1544-7 (*see also* Plate CXL).

(V.99)

Bucklers.

Plate CXXXVIII

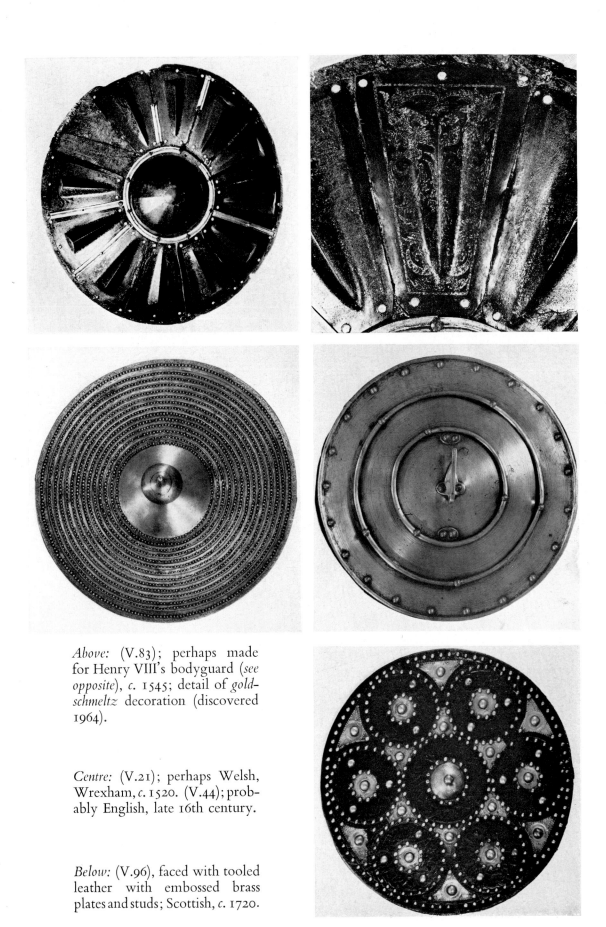

Above: (V.83); perhaps made for Henry VIII's bodyguard (*see opposite*), *c.* 1545; detail of *gold-schmeltz* decoration (discovered 1964).

Centre: (V.21); perhaps Welsh, Wrexham, *c.* 1520. (V.44); probably English, late 16th century.

Below: (V.96), faced with tooled leather with embossed brass plates and studs; Scottish, *c.* 1720.

Bucklers and targe, 16th–18th century.

PLATE CXXXIX

Detail of engraving discovered in 1964, depicting legend of Mucius Scævola, on 'gun-shield' (V. 39), made probably by Giovanbattista and company of Ravenna (*see* Plate CXXXVIII); *c.* 1544–7.

Plate CXL

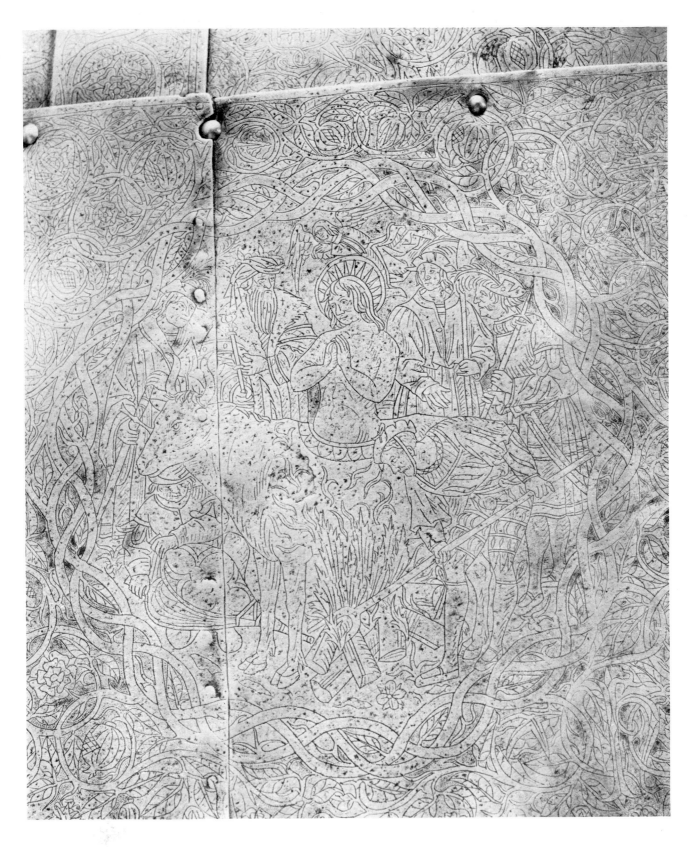

Bard (VI. 1–5) of Henry VIII's silvered armour; detail of engraving by Paul van Vrelant showing St. George being boiled in a brazen ox; *c.* 1514–9 (*see also* Plate I).

PLATE CXLI

Shield (V. 17), of embossed leather, with opening for lantern; Italian, late 16th century.

Shield (V. 16), (inside) painted with scenes from life of Camillus; Italian, mid 16th century.

PLATE CXLII

Shield (V. 97), of steel etched and gilt, with fringe of green silk; German, dated 1603.

PLATE CXLIII

Horse chanfrons, 15th century.

(VI. 323); probably German, *c.* 1480. From Rhodes.

Below (VI. 375), front view, and lining; Innsbruck, *c.* 1470.

inside showing original canvas From Armoury at Churburg.

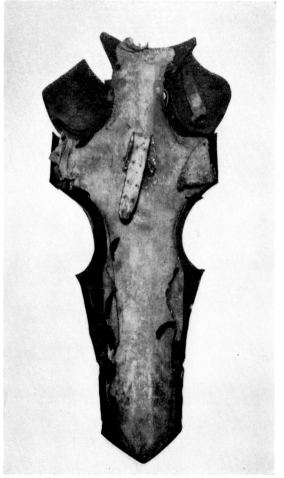

PLATE CXLIV

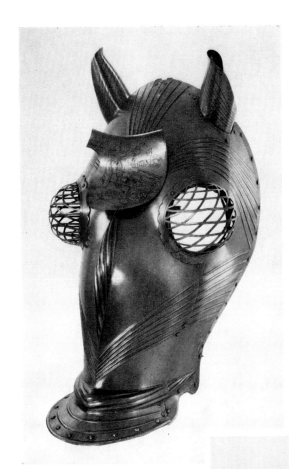

(VI. 368); German, *c.* 1515.

(V. 369); German, probably Nuremberg, *c.* 1520.

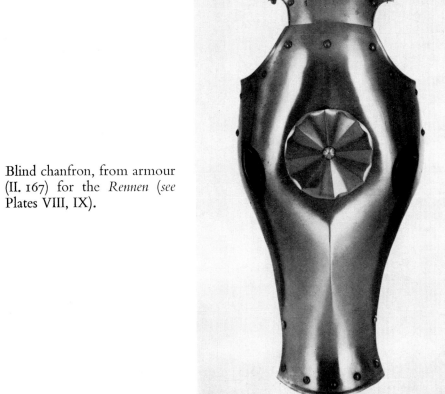

Blind chanfron, from armour (II. 167) for the *Rennen* (*see* Plates VIII, IX).

Horse chanfrons, late 15th – early 16th century.

PLATE CXLV

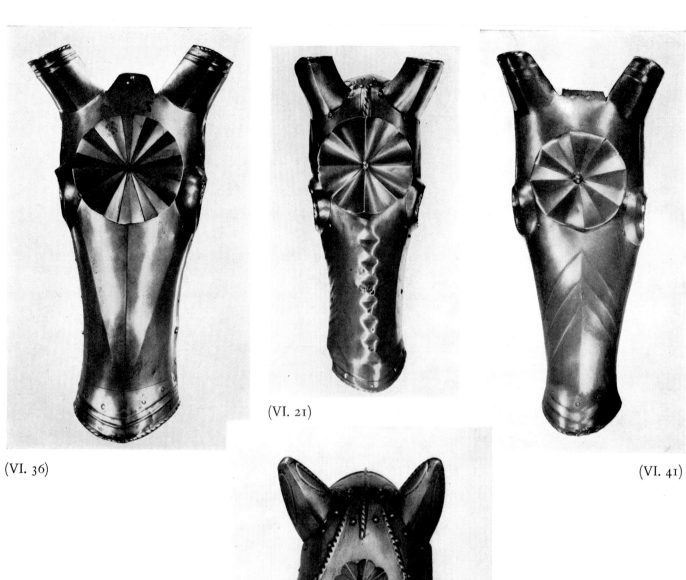

(VI. 36)

(VI. 21)

(VI. 41)

Horse armour: munition chanfrons; probably Flemish, *c.* 1520–30.

(VI. 35)

PLATE CXLVI

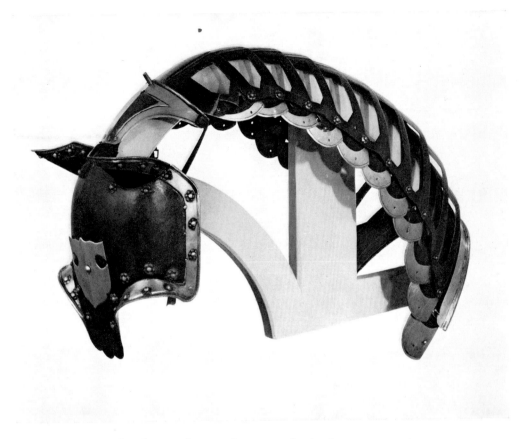

Chanfron and crinet (VI. 56 and 67); German, *c.* 1560.

Horse armour.

Peytral (VI. 74) and crupper (VI. 82); European, early 16th century.

PLATE CXLVII

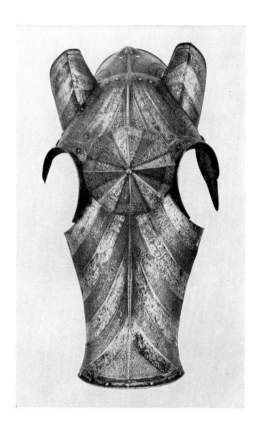

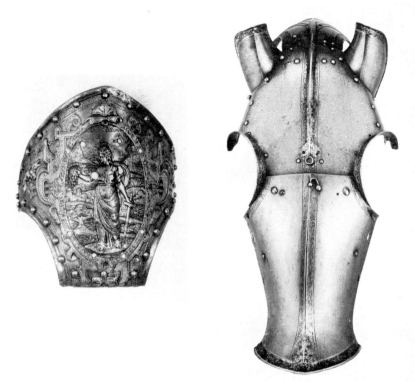

Above left: (VI. 55), probably from armour of Henry VIII; made in Royal Workshops at Greenwich, *c.* 1535.

Middle: (VI. 25), top plate of chanfron, embossed and gilt; Flemish, *c.* 1570.

Above right: (VI. 13), probably from armour of Henry VIII; made in Royal Workshops at Greenwich, *c.* 1540.

Chanfrons etc., 16th century.

Below: (VI. 370), half chanfron bearing the arms of Schellendorf, probably for Carl Magnus Schellendorf (1562–1621); German, *c.* 1600.

PLATE CXLVIII

Above: (VI. 60) belonging to armour (II. 91) of King Charles I (*see* Plate L); French or English, *c.* 1625.

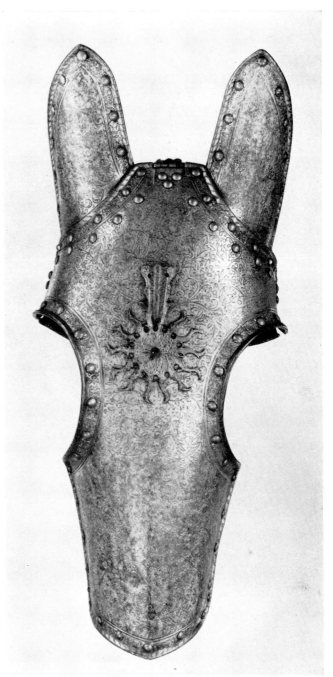

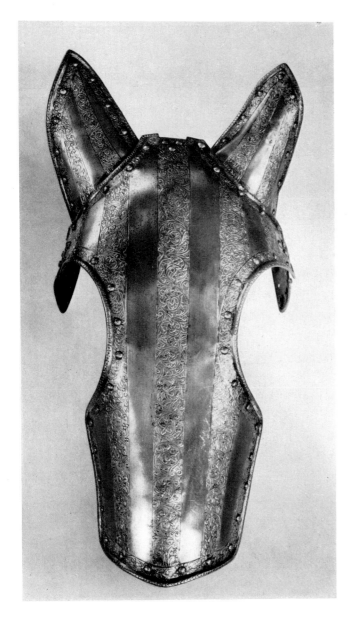

Chanfrons, 17th century.

Below: (VI. 59) belonging to armour (II. 90) of Prince Charles, later Charles II (*see* Plate LIII); French or English, *c.* 1645.

PLATE CXLIX

Horse armour (VI. 6–12), known as the 'Burgundian bard', embossed with
crosses and firesteels of the Order of the Golden Fleece; mark stamped on
crupper; probably Flemish, *c.* 1510.

Plate CL

Horse armour (VI. 18–20), with etched bands; North Italian, *c.* 1580.

PLATE CLI

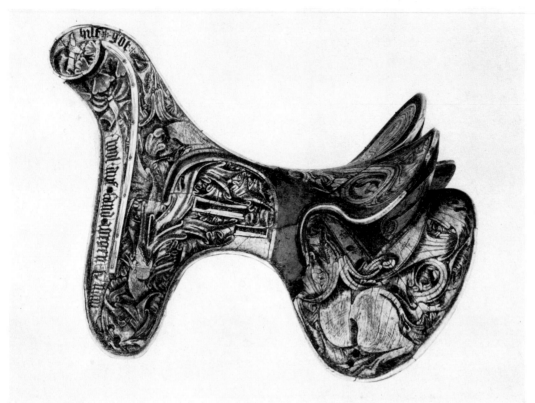

Near side.

Saddle (VI. 95), of wood overlaid with engraved and coloured stag horn; German, late 15th century.

Off side.

PLATE CLII

Back, from above.

Near side.

Saddle (VI. 94), for German form of joust known as *Hohenzeuggestech*; German, 15th century.

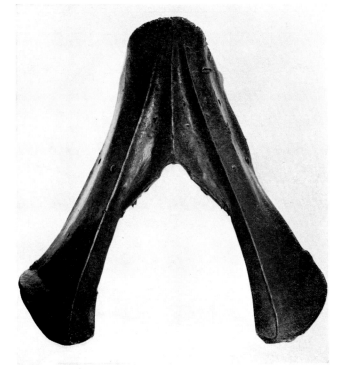

Front.

Saddle (VI. 366), with defensive plates, saddle-tree lined with birch bark; German, early 16th century.

PLATE CLIII

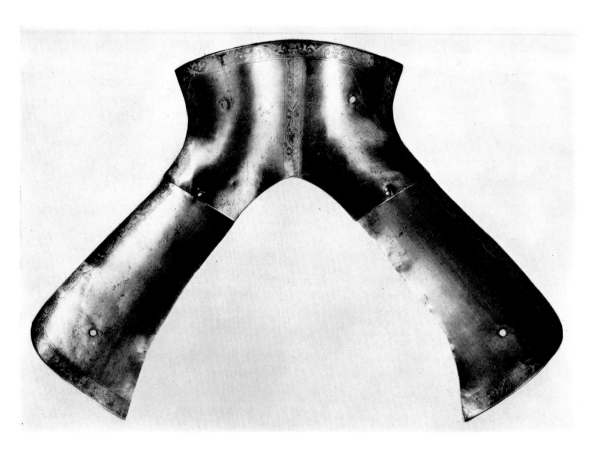

Saddle steels (VI. 99), made in Royal Workshops at Greenwich, probably for King Henry VIII, *c.* 1540.

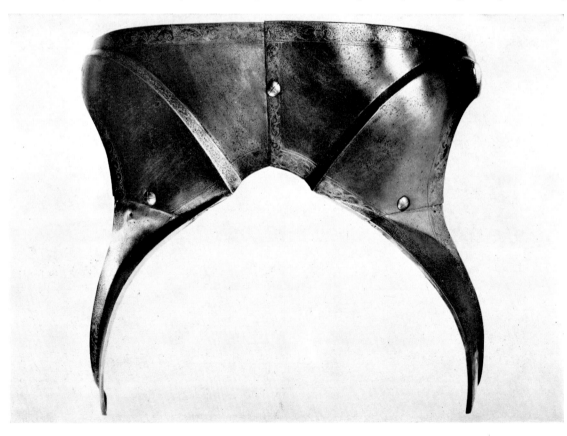

PLATE CLIV

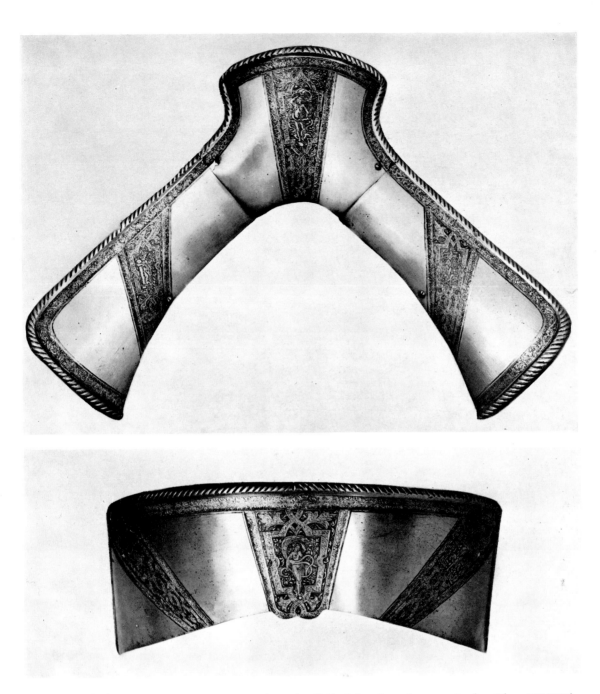

Saddle steels from an armour garniture (II. 84) of Sir John Smythe, *c.* 1585 (*see* Plate XLVIII).

Detail of etched and gilt decoration of steels (VI. 99) *opposite*.

PLATE CLV

Tail defence (VI. 319) from lost horse armour, embossed as monstrous mask; by Kunz Lochner of Nuremberg, c. 1530.

Saddle steel (VI. 111), part only, freely pierced, engraved and gilt; probably Flemish, c. 1545.

Stirrups *below*: (VI. 327, *left*), of brass cast in relief, enamelled and gilt; English, c. 1660; (VI. 155, *right*), of cast bronze, formerly gilt; early 17th century.

PLATE CLVI

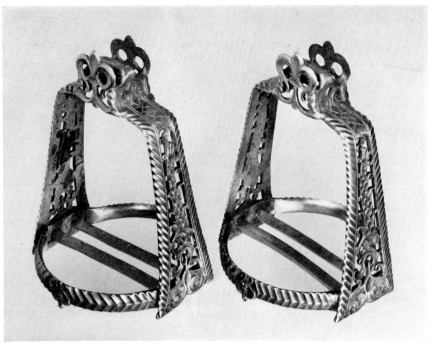

(VI. 347, *above left*), of chiselled steel; 16th century. (VI. 142–3, *above*) of chiselled steel *en suite* with bit (VI. 229, *see* Plate CLIX); late 16th century. (VI. 153–4, *left*), of steel engraved and gilt; probably English, *c.* 1600.

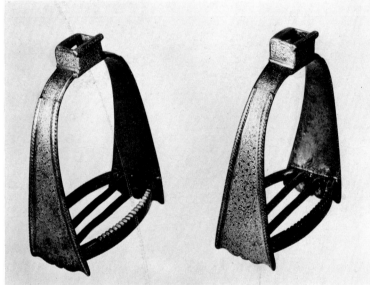

Stirrups.

(VI. 194) box stirrup; probably Spanish, late 17th or early 18th century.

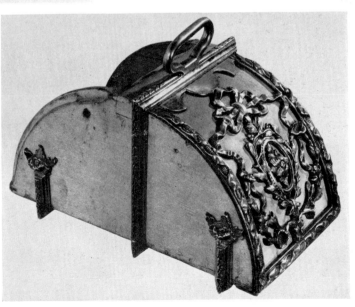

PLATE CLVII

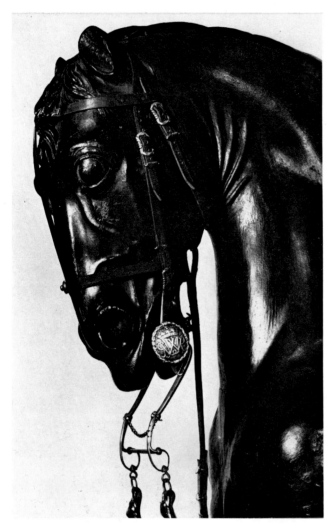

(VI. 199), made for Bürgermeister Johannes Welser of Augsburg, dated 1572.

(VI. 222), with cast brass bosses displaying monogram of William III; English, *c.* 1700.

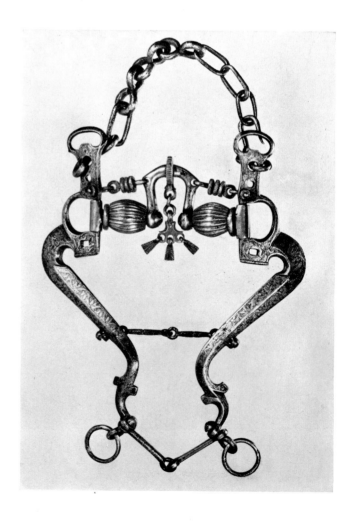

(VI. 200), etched and gilt; probably English, early 16th century.

Horse harness: bits and **muzzle.**

PLATE CLVIII

(VI. 229), of chiselled steel, *en suite* with stirrups
(VI. 142–3, *see* Plate CLVII); late 16th century.

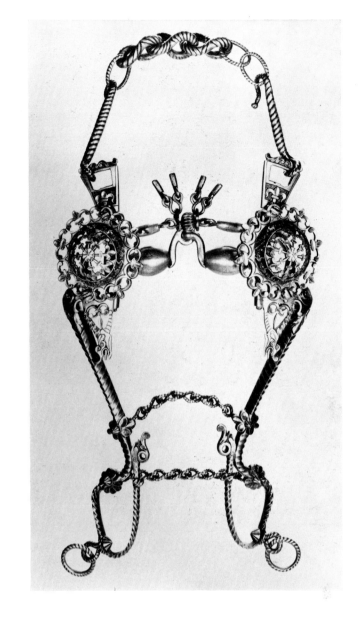

(VI. 327a), with brass bosses cast in relief and
enamelled; English, *c.* 1660.

Horse harness: bits.

PLATE CLIX

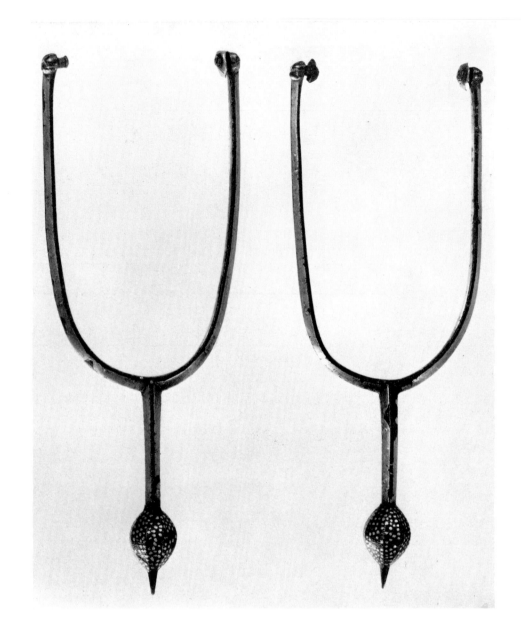

Prick spurs.
Above: (VI. 373–4), of iron, embellished with gold and silver sheeting and dots; early 11th century. From tomb in church of St. Andrew, Chardstock, Devon. *Below:* (VI. 380), fragment, of bronze; first half of 13th century. Found in London.

PLATE CLX

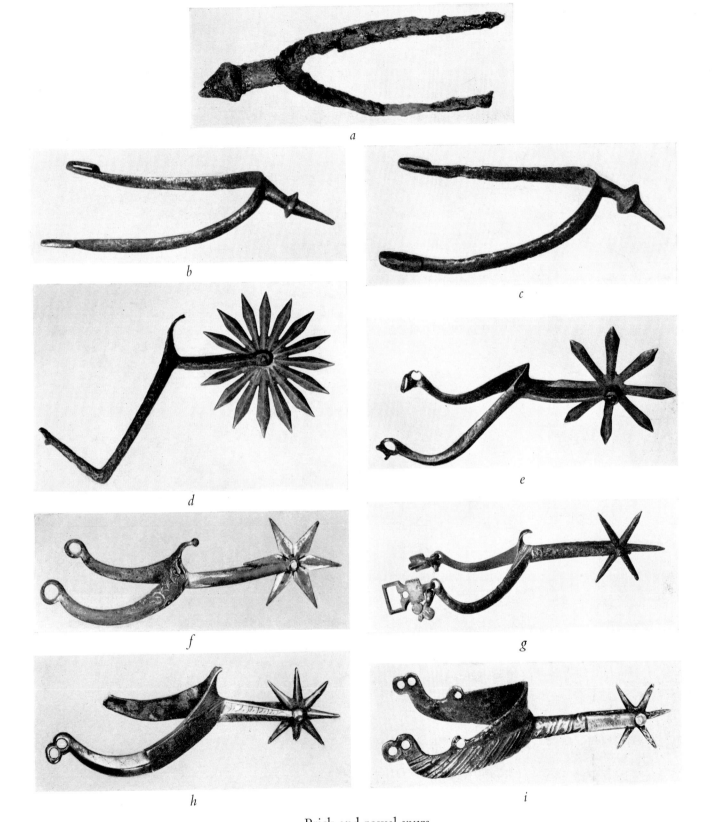

Prick and rowel spurs.
(*a*) (VI. 238), of iron; 11th or 12th century.　(*b*) (VI. 331), of iron; 13th century.
(*c*) (VI. 332), of iron; 13th century.　(*d*) (VI. 350), of iron with bronze rowel;
c. 1350.　(*e*) (VI. 358), of bronze; *c.* 1370.　(*f*) (VI. 365), of copper gilt; *c.* 1400.
(*g*) (VI. 342), one of pair, of copper gilt; *c.* 1400.　(*h*) (VI. 386), of bronze; early
15th century.　(*i*) (VI. 361), of steel; German, *c.* 1500.

PLATE CLXI

(VI. 381), of bronze, engraved with scale pattern and flowers and retaining traces of gilding; *c.* 1400. Found in moat of Tower of London when drained in 1843.

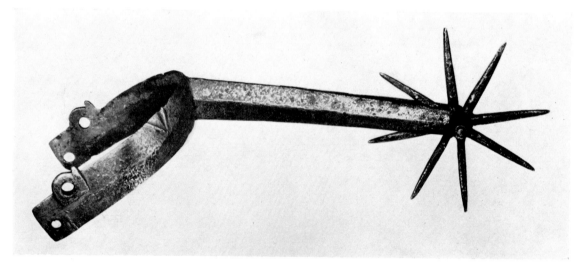

(VI. 363), of steel; German, late 15th century.

(VI. 382), of steel sheathed in brass; German, *c.* 1490–1500. From Vienna, said to have belonged to Emperor Maximilian I.

Rowel spurs, 15th century.

PLATE CLXII

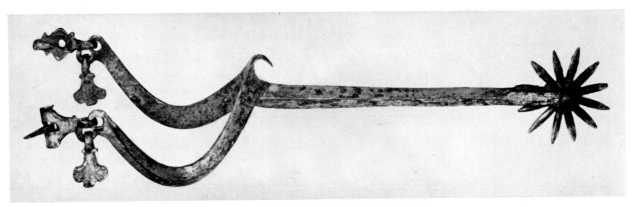

(VI. 322), one of pair, of iron; probably Italian, second half of 15th century.

(VI. 371), one of pair, of iron sheathed in engraved brass; German, *c.* 1490.

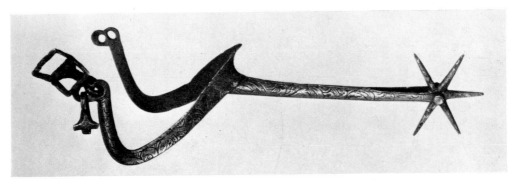

(VI. 334), of iron, engraved; German, second half of 15th century.

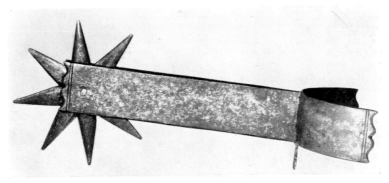

(VI. 364), of iron, screwed to heel of boot; probably Hungarian, second half of 16th century.

Rowel spurs. 15th and 16th century.

PLATE CLXIII

a

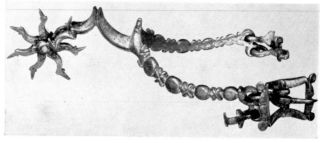

b

d

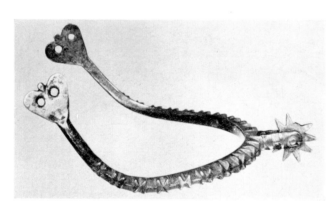

c

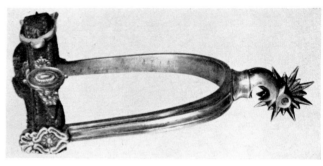

f

e

Rowel spurs, 17th and 18th century.

(*a*) (VI. 352), of iron with applied silver decoration; English, *c*. 1620.   (*b*) (VI. 354), one of pair; European, *c*. 1630.   (*c*) (VI. 387), of bronze; European, mid 17th century.   (*d*) (VI. 388); European, mid 17th century. (*e*) (VI. 313); European, 17th century.   (*f*) (VI. 305), of silver-plated brass, retaining original leathers and buckles; European, 18th century. (*g*) (VI. 338), to grip heel of shoe; probably English, mid 17th century.

g

PLATE CLXIV

TABLE OF INVENTORY AND
PLATE NUMBERS

Inventory Numbers	Plate Numbers	Inventory Numbers	Plate Numbers
I.36	XLVII	II.124	LXVI
I.39	LII	II.126	LXVIII
I.41	LXXI	II.135	XVII
I.46	XXXIX	II.137	XXXVIII
I.47	CXXIV	II.138	LXIII
I.49	LVIII	II.139	LXV
I.50	CXXX	II.140	LXX
I.54	XXX	II.141	LXII
		II.145	XXXV
		II.146	LX, LXI
II.1	VI, CXXVII	II.160	LXIX
II.2	V, XCI	II.161	LXIX
II.3	II, LXXIX	II.162	LXIII
II.4	XVII	II.163	LXVIII
II.5	I, XIV, XV, LXXXI, CXLI	II.164	LXII
II.6	XII, XIII, LXXXVII	II.167	VIII, IX, CXXXIII, CXLV
II.7	X, XI	II.168	VII, LXXVI
II.8	Frontis., IV, XVIII–XXIII	II.169	XXXII
II.10	CXXVIII, CXXIX	II.170	LVII
II.11	CXIII	II.171	XVI
II.12	XCII	II.172	XXIX, CXXXII
II.14	XC	II.173	XXVIII
II.16	CXV	II.176	LXX
II.18	CXV	II.178	XXXVI, XXXVII
II.22	XXIV	II.179	XVI
II.23	XXV	II.180	LXI
II.25	LX	II.182	CI
II.27	CXXIII	II.183	XXXIII
II.29	XXIV	II.184	LVI
II.31	XXV	II.185	LVI
II.33	XXV, C	II.186	LIV, LV, CI
II.40	XLVI	II.187	XXXI
II.42	LIX	II.188	XXXIV
II.47	LIX		
II.74	LVII	III.9	CXXVI
II.78	XCV	III.47	CXXIII
II.80	LII	III.71	CX
II.81	XLIV, XLV, XCIV	III.75	CXIII
II.82	XL	III.85	CXII
II.83	XLI, XLII, XLIII	III.94–5	CXV
II.84	XLVIII, XLIX, XCVIII, XCIX, CLV	III.99	CXVII
		III.100	CXVIII
II.85	CXXXI	III.104	CXVII
II.88	XXVI, XXVII	III.117	CXVI
II.89	XXVI, XXVII, XCVI	III.118	CXVII
II.90	LIII	III.127	CXX
II.91	L, LI	III.148	CXXI
II.92	LI, LXVI	III.250	CXX
II.108	CXX	III.400	CXXI
II.112	LXIV	III.429	CXXI
II.117	LXV	III.736–7	CXXXII
II.123	LXVII	III.771–2	CXXXII

Inventory Numbers	Plate Numbers	Inventory Numbers	Plate Numbers
III.773	CXXII	IV.9	LXXVIII
III.782–3	CXXII	IV.12	LXXIX
III.792	CXXII	IV.16	LXXIX
III.813	CXXII	IV.17	LXXIV
III.850	CXXXV	IV.18	LXXV
III.874	CXXXIII	IV.20	LXXVII
III.905	CXX	IV.22	LXXXII
III.1011–2	VI	IV.24	LXXXIX
III.1027	CXXI	IV.26	LXXXIX
III.1031	CXXI	IV.29	XC
III.1058	CXIX	IV.33	XCII
III.1083	VI	IV.36	LXXXIX
III.1086	CXIII	IV.39	LXXXVII
III.1087	CXII	IV.41	XCIV
III.1090	CXIII	IV.43	XCV
III.1092	CX	IV.48	CVII
III.1093	CXI	IV.51	C
III.1122–3	VI	IV.72	LIX
III.1157	CXXV	IV.143	CII
III.1165	CXXII	IV.144	CIII
III.1167	LXV	IV.154	XCVII
III.1197–8	CXXIII	IV.156	CVI
III.1214	CXXII	IV.159	CV
III.1218	CXVII	IV.164	XCIII
III.1226	CXXV	IV.165	CV
III.1227	CVIII	IV.166	CVI
III.1228	CVIII	IV.174	CV
III.1246	CXII	IV.185	CV
III.1251	CXVIII	IV.211	CV
III.1252	CXXVI	IV.333	CXXXIV
III.1264	CXXII	IV.350	CIV
III.1265	CXXXIII	IV.411	LXXXVI
III.1277	CXXIII	IV.412	XC
III.1279	CXXVI	IV.413	LXXXVIII
III.1280	CXXVI	IV.414	C
III.1282	CIX	IV.416	C
III.1283	CXI	IV.417	CIV
III.1284	CIX	IV.420	CII
III.1285–6	CXXVII	IV.424	LXXVII
III.1287	CX	IV.425	LXXVII
III.1288–9	CXIV, CXV	IV.427	LXXIX
III.1293–4	CXI	IV.429	LXXIX
III.1297	CXVI	IV.430	LXXX
III.1300	CXXIII	IV.433	CII
III.1301	CXXV	IV.443	CIV
III.1319	CXXXII	IV.449	CII
III.1320	CXXVI	IV.453	LXXVII
III.1321	LXXIX	IV.467	LXXIII
III.1325	CX	IV.468	LXXX
III.1327	CXX	IV.470	LXXII
III.1328	CXIX	IV.471	XCI
III.1329	CXVIII	IV.472	XC
III.1336	CXIX	IV.474	XCIII
III.1338	CXVI	IV.476	XCIII
III.1341	CXXI	IV.477	CXXXV
III.1342	CXXI	IV.485	CVI
		IV.490	LXXVIII
IV.1	LXXXIII	IV.498	LXXXI
IV.2	LXXXV	IV.499	LXXIX
IV.6	LXXIII	IV.500	LXXVIII, CXXIII
IV.7	LXXIV	IV.501	XCII
IV.8	LXXV	IV.502	LXXXIV

Inventory Numbers	Plate Numbers	Inventory Numbers	Plate Numbers
IV.503	CIII	VI.67	CXLVII
IV.505	XCIII	VI.74	CXLVII
IV.506	CVII	VI.77	V
IV.512	CIII	VI.82	CXLVII
IV.516	CVII	VI.84	V
IV.518	CIII	VI.94	CLIII
IV.519	CV	VI.95	CLII
IV.520	CXXXIV	VI.96–7	IV
IV.521	LXXXIX	VI.99	CLIV, CLV
IV.522	CVI	VI.111	CLVI
IV.523	CIV	VI.142–3	CLVII
IV.524	CVII	VI.153–4	CLVII
IV.525	CII	VI.155	CLVI
IV.526	CIII	VI.194	CLVII
IV.529	CIV	VI.199	CLVIII
		VI.200	CLVIII
V.1	CXXXVI	VI.222	CLVIII
V.2	CXXXVI	VI.229	CLIX
V.3	CXXXVII	VI.238	CLXI
V.6	CXXXVII	VI.305	CLXIV
V.7	CXXXVI	VI.313	CLXIV
V.10	CXXXVII	VI.319	CLVI
V.13	CXXXVI	VI.322	CLXIII
V.16	CXLII	VI.323	CXLIV
V.17	CXLII	VI.327	CLVI
V.21	CXXXIX	VI.327a	CLIX
V.37	CXXXVIII	VI.331	CLXI
V.39	CXL	VI.332	CLXI
V.43	CXXXVIII	VI.334	CLXIII
V.44	CXXXIX	VI.338	CLXIV
V.81	CXXXVIII	VI.342	CLXI
V.83	CXXXIX	VI.347	CLVII
V.96	CXXXIX	VI.348	CXXXIV
V.97	CXLIII	VI.350	CLXI
V.98	CXXXVII	VI.352	CLXIV
V.99	CXXXVIII	VI.354	CLXIV
		VI.358	CLXI
		VI.361	CLXI
VI.1–5	I	VI.363	CLXII
VI.6–12	CL	VI.364	CLXIII
VI.13–16	IV, CXLVIII	VI.365	CLXI
VI.18–20	CLI	VI.366	CLIII
VI.21	CXLVI	VI.368	CXLV
VI.25	CXLVIII	VI.369	CXLV
VI.34	V	VI.370	CXLVIII
VI.35	CXLVI	VI.371	CLXIII
VI.36	CXLVI	VI.373–4	CLX
VI.41	CXLVI	VI.375	CXLIV
VI.49	XLV	VI.379	II, III
VI.50	XLIII	VI.380	CLX
VI.51	XLIX	VI.381	CLXII
VI.52	CXXXI	VI.382	CLXII
VI.55	CXLVIII	VI.386	CLXI
VI.56	CXLVII	VI.387	CLXIV
VI.59	CXLIX	VI.388	CLXIV
VI.60	CXLIX		
VI.65	V	XIII.119	CXXV

INDEX

(References to the Introduction are in Arabic numerals,
to the plates in Roman numerals.)

Printed in England for Her Majesty's Stationery Office by Waterlow & Sons Limited · London · Dunstable · Hyde.

Wt. 3614 K40

S.O. Code No. 67—164•